EXODUS

Chapters 19—40

J. Vernon McGee

THOMAS NELSON PUBLISHERS

Nashville • Atlanta • London • Vancouver

Published in Nashville, Tennessee, by Thomas Nelson, Inc.

Scripture quotations are from the KING JAMES VERSION of the Bible.

Library of Congress Cataloging-in-Publication Data

McGee, J. Vernon (John Vernon), 1904–1988
   [Thru the Bible with J. Vernon McGee]
   Thru the Bible commentary series / J. Vernon McGee.
     p.   cm.
   Reprint. Originally published: Thru the Bible with J. Vernon McGee. 1975.
   Includes bibliographical references.
   ISBN 0-7852-1005-9 (TR)
   ISBN 0-7852-1071-7 (NRM)
   1. Bible—Commentaries. I. Title.
BS491.2.M37 1991
220.7'7—dc20   90–41340
                                                        CIP

Printed in the United States of America
4 5 6 7 8 9 — 99 98 97 96

CONTENTS

EXODUS—Chapters 19—40

PREFACE

The radio broadcasts of the Thru the Bible Radio five-year program were transcribed, edited, and published first in single-volume paperbacks to accommodate the radio audience.

There has been a minimal amount of further editing for this publication. Therefore, these messages are not the word-for-word recording of the taped messages which went out over the air. The changes were necessary to accommodate a reading audience rather than a listening audience.

These are popular messages, prepared originally for a radio audience. They should not be considered a commentary on the entire Bible in any sense of that term. These messages are devoid of any attempt to present a theological or technical commentary on the Bible. Behind these messages is a great deal of research and study in order to interpret the Bible from a popular rather than from a scholarly (and too-often boring) viewpoint.

We have definitely and deliberately attempted "to put the cookies on the bottom shelf so that the kiddies could get them."

The fact that these messages have been translated into many languages for radio broadcasting and have been received with enthusiasm reveals the need for a simple teaching of the whole Bible for the masses of the world.

I am indebted to many people and to many sources for bringing this volume into existence. I should express my especial thanks to my secretary, Gertrude Cutler, who supervised the editorial work; to Dr. Elliott R. Cole, my associate, who handled all the detailed work with the publishers; and finally, to my wife Ruth for tenaciously encouraging me from the beginning to put my notes and messages into printed form.

Solomon wrote, ". . . of making many books there is no end; and much study is a weariness of the flesh" (Eccl. 12:12). On a sea of books that flood the marketplace, we launch this series of THRU THE BIBLE with the hope that it might draw many to the one Book, *The Bible*.

J. VERNON MCGEE

The Book of
EXODUS

INTRODUCTION

Exodus continues the account which was begun in Genesis, although there was a lapse of at least 3½ centuries. Genesis 15:13 says that the seed of Abraham would spend 400 years in Egypt. Exodus 12:40 says that it was 430 years, and Galatians 3:16–17 confirms it. It was 430 years from the call of Abraham, and 400 years from the time that God told Abraham.

Exodus means "the way out" and tells the story of redemption by blood and by power. The message of Exodus is stated in Hebrews 11:23–29, which says: "By faith Moses, when he was born, was hid three months of his parents, because they saw he was a proper child; and they were not afraid of the king's commandment. By faith Moses, when he was come to years, refused to be called the son of Pharaoh's daughter; choosing rather to suffer affliction with the people of God, than to enjoy the pleasures of sin for a season; esteeming the reproach of Christ greater riches than the treasures in Egypt: for he had respect unto the recompense of the reward. By faith he forsook Egypt, not fearing the wrath of the king: for he endured, as seeing him who is invisible. Through faith he kept the passover, and the sprinkling of blood, lest he that destroyed the firstborn should touch them. By faith they passed through the Red sea as by dry land: which the Egyptians assaying to do were drowned."

The word which opens Exodus is a conjunction that is better translated *and* rather than *now*. Exodus has been called the sequel to Genesis. Dr. G. Campbell Morgan wrote, "In the Book of Exodus nothing is commenced, nothing is finished."

Genesis 46:27 tells us that seventy souls of Jacob entered Egypt. It is conservatively estimated that 2,100,000 left Egypt at the time of the Exodus. Although it is impossible to be certain about dates in this early period, it would seem that Joseph entered Egypt under the Hyksos or shepherd kings who were Semitic conquerors, and were related to Abraham, Isaac, and Jacob. Actually the Israelites may have been their only friends, as they were hated by Egyptians. Finally they were driven out by a native Egyptian dynasty which was understandably hostile to foreigners. In this line was the Pharaoh of the oppression and the one "who knew not Joseph."

Moses figures prominently in the Book of Exodus. He is the author of the Pentateuch which includes the first five books of the Old Testament—Genesis, Exodus, Leviticus, Numbers, and Deuteronomy. In the Book of Exodus, Moses' life is divided into three forty-year periods:

1. Forty years in Pharaoh's palace in Egypt
2. Forty years in the desert in Midian
3. Forty years in the wilderness as leader of Israel

Moses' training in Egypt, evidently in the Temple of the Sun, did not prepare him to follow God in leading Israel out of Egypt. God trained him in the desert for forty years to reveal to him that he could *not* deliver Israel alone. God gave Moses a B.D. (Backside of the Desert) degree.

It should be noted that after God prepared Moses to deliver his people, He sent him back to Egypt after forty years. Moses is to assemble elders of Israel and go to Pharaoh. Pharaoh will refuse to let Israel go. His refusal will open the contest between God and the gods of Egypt. Egypt was dominated by idolatry—"gods many and lords many." There were thousands of temples and millions of idols. Behind idolatry was Satan. There was *power* in the religion of Egypt—"Now as Jannes and Jambres withstood Moses, so do these also resist the truth: men of corrupt minds, reprobate concerning the faith" (2 Tim. 3:8). Pharaoh asked, ". . . Who is the LORD, that I should obey his voice to let Israel go? I know not the LORD, neither will I let Israel go" (Exod. 5:2). God introduced Himself. Pharaoh got acquainted with God and acknowledged Him as God. "And Pharaoh sent, and called for Moses and Aaron, and said unto them, I have sinned this time: the LORD is righteous, and I and my people are wicked" (Exod. 9:27). "Then Pharaoh called for Moses and Aaron in haste; and he said, I have sinned against the LORD your God, and against you" (Exod. 10:16).

A question arises from this episode: Why the plagues? They were God's battle with the gods of Egypt. Each plague was directed against a particular god in Egypt. "For I will pass through the land of Egypt this night, and will smite all the firstborn in the land of Egypt, both man and beast; and against all the gods of Egypt I will execute judgment: I am the LORD" (Exod. 12:12). God wanted to reveal to His own people that He, the LORD, was far greater than any god of Egypt and that He had power to deliver them.

OUTLINE

I. A Deliverer, Chapters 1—11
A. Slavery of Israel in Egypt, Chapter 1
B. Birth of Moses—First Forty Years in Pharaoh's Palace, Chapter 2
C. Call of Moses—Second Forty Years in Midian, Chapter 3
   (Incident of burning bush)
D. Return of Moses to Egypt—Announcement of Deliverance to Israel, Chapter 4
E. Contest with Pharaoh, Chapters 5—11
   (9 plagues against idolatry of Egypt, battle of the gods)

II. Deliverance (by Blood and Power), Chapters 12—14
A. Institution of Passover—Tenth Plague, Death of Firstborn (Blood), Chapter 12
B. Crossing Red Sea—Destruction of Army of Egypt (Power), Chapters 13—14

III. Marching to Mount Sinai (Spiritual Education), Chapters 15—18
   (7 experiences correspond to Christian experience)
A. Song of Redeemed—Wilderness of Shur, Chapter 15:1-22
   (No bed of roses after redemption)
B. Marah, Bitter Water Sweetened by Tree, Chapter 15:23-26
   (Cross sweetens bitter experiences of life)
C. Elim (Fruitful Christian Experience), Chapter 15:27
D. Wilderness of Sin—Manna and Quail, Chapter 16
   (Christ is the Bread of Life.)
E. Smitten Rock ("That Rock was Christ"), Chapter 17:1-7
F. Amalek (the Flesh), Chapter 17:8-16
   (Victory on the hill top, Deut. 25:17-18)
G. Jethro, Priest of Midian, Chapter 18
   (Worldly wisdom in contrast to revelation)

CHAPTER 19

THEME: Moses delivers God's message; Israel prepares for a visitation from God

Chapters 19 through 24 deal with the Law. The children of Israel have arrived at Mount Sinai, and here they agree to accept the Law. In fact, what they do is exchange grace for law.

> In the third month, when the children of Israel were gone forth out of the land of Egypt, the same day came they into the wilderness of Sinai.
>
> For they were departed from Rephidim, and were come to the desert of Sinai, and had pitched in the wilderness; and there Israel camped before the mount [Exod. 19:1-2].

The children of Israel have arrived at Mount Sinai, the place where the Law is going to be given. God is going to deal graciously with His people. He is going to give them the opportunity of deciding whether they want to go on with God leading them—the way He has for the period of time since they left Egypt until they arrived at the mount—or whether they would rather accept and receive the Law.

MOSES DELIVERS GOD'S MESSAGE

> And Moses went up unto God, and the LORD called unto him out of the mountain, saying, Thus shalt thou say to the house of Jacob, and tell the children of Israel; Ye have seen what I did unto the Egyptians, and how I bare you on eagles' wings, and brought you unto myself [Exod. 19:3-4].

That's traveling by grace!

**Now therefore, if ye will obey my voice indeed, and keep
my covenant, then ye shall be a peculiar treasure unto
me above all people: for all the earth is mine [Exod.
19:5].**

The children of Israel traveled from Egypt to Mount Sinai by the grace
of God. Then God asks them if they want to receive the Law and commandments, and they foolishly agree to accept it instead of saying that
they enjoyed the trip on eagles' wings from Egypt to Mount Sinai.

God reminded them of what He had done to the Egyptians and
how He had borne the children of Israel on eagles' wings. Perhaps a
few words should be said about the eagle. The eagle is a bird of prey,
which Job 9:26 corroborates by saying, "They are passed away as the
swift ships: as the eagle that hasteth to the prey." The Lord Jesus Christ
Himself said, "For wheresoever the carcase is, there will the eagles be
gathered together" (Matt. 24:28). Yet the eagle is used as a symbol of
God and deity in Scripture. In the Book of Ezekiel deity is represented
by the face of an eagle. In the fourth chapter of the Book of Revelation
deity is pictured by a flying eagle. The eagle is admired for its wings
and its ability to soar to the heights. In other words, the eagle is the jet
plane of the bird family, and the wings of the eagle are definitely a
symbol of deity. God said to Israel in Exodus 19:4, "Ye have seen what
I did unto the Egyptians, and how I bare you on eagles' wings, and
brought you unto myself." That, friends, is God's marvelous, infinite,
wonderful grace. By grace God brought Israel out of Egypt and to
Mount Sinai. God had found them helpless and hopeless in the slavery of Egypt, and He delivered them. He redeemed them by blood.
The same night the death angel passed over, the children of Israel
marched out of Egypt. They came to the Red Sea where Pharaoh could
have slaughtered them like animals, but God intervened. And God
brought them across the Red Sea by power. You see, He is bearing
them on eagles' wings.

On the way from Egypt to Mount Sinai, Israel had seven experiences which correspond to our Christian experiences. God gave Israel manna when they were hungry and water when they were thirsty. God sweetened the bitter waters of Marah. God delivered them from Amalek. All the way God bore Israel on eagles' wings, and that is the way He bears us today. He leads us by His grace, and we walk by faith.

Now at Mount Sinai God reminds Israel how He has led and cared for them. Then He gives them a choice—grace or law. God asks them if they will keep the commandments if He gives them to Israel. They are going to exchange grace for law. A great many people do that today. This is unfortunate because we live in a day when God saves by grace. God does not save by law. What a contrast there is between law and grace.

Law demands—grace gives.

Law says "do"—grace says "believe."

Law exacts—grace bestows.

Law says "work"—grace says "rest."

Law threatens, pronouncing a curse—grace entreats, pronouncing a blessing.

Law says "Do, and thou shalt live"—grace says, "Live, and thou shalt do."

Law condemns the best man—grace saves the worst man.

The Law reveals the character of God—it also reveals the weakness of man. In Romans 3:19 Paul says, "Now we know that what things soever the law saith, it saith to them who are under the law: that every mouth may be stopped, and all the world may become guilty before God."

God never gave the Law as a means of salvation. No one was ever saved by keeping the Law. You can't mention a single one. Moses was a murderer; he also lost his temper and disobeyed God. Why then was the Law given? There was a definite reason which is stated in Galatians 3:19—"Wherefore then serveth the law? It was added because of transgressions, till the seed should come to whom the promise was made. . . ." The law was given to reveal that we are sinners. It was given temporarily until the Seed would come. The seed spoken of in this verse is the Lord Jesus Christ. Paul goes on to say in Galatians 3:24 that, ". . . the law was our schoolmaster to bring us unto Christ, that we might be justified by faith."

The "schoolmaster" is not a school teacher, but a slave in the home of a Roman patrician that took care of the child. He clothed, washed, dressed him, blew his nose when needed, and paddled him when necessary. When the child was old enough to attend school, the schoolmaster took him. The word for schoolmaster is *paidagōgos*, meaning a "child conductor," one who takes a little child by the hand and leads him to the school. The Law is our schoolmaster, our *paidagōgos*. It takes us by the hand, like a little child, and leads us to the Cross and says, "My little one, you need a Savior. You are a sinner and you need to be saved."

> **And ye shall be unto me a kingdom of priests, and an holy nation. These are the words which thou shalt speak unto the children of Israel [Exod. 19:6].**

God originally intended for Israel to be a kingdom of priests. All of the tribes were to be priests. Because of their failure to enter the land at Kadesh-barnea and because they made and worshiped a golden calf while Moses was on the mountain receiving God's law, only one tribe was chosen to be a priestly tribe. God's ultimate goal in the Millennium, however, is to make the entire nation a kingdom of priests. This will happen long after the church is removed from this earth and is in heaven with the Lord Jesus Christ in the New Jerusalem.

> **And Moses came and called for the elders of the people, and laid before their faces all these words which the LORD commanded him [Exod. 19:7].**

Listen to these people—what confidence they had!

> **And all the people answered together, and said, All that the LORD hath spoken we will do. And Moses returned the words of the people unto the LORD [Exod. 19:8].**

The giving of the Law to the nation Israel at Mount Sinai was the beginning of the dispensation of Law. This dispensation extends from Mount Sinai to the Cross of Calvary, from the Exodus to the Cross. It is the revelation to a people, living under ideal conditions, that they cannot keep the Law. Israel said, "All that the Lord hath spoken *we will do*." They said, "Bring it on; we'll keep it" before they even knew what it was! Then they demonstrated for fifteen hundred years that they could not keep the Law. This is the attitude of a great many people today—they think the natural man can please God. The natural man cannot keep the Law and he fails terribly in the attempt. The Law was given to control the old nature but it cannot, because the old nature is a revolutionary which cannot be controlled. Paul sums it up in Romans 8:6–7 like this, "For to be carnally minded is death; but to be spiritually minded is life and peace. Because the carnal mind is enmity against God: for it is not subject to the law of God, neither indeed can be."

You and I have an old nature. It is at enmity with God. It can never be obedient to God and can never please Him. Have you made that discovery in your own life? Have you found that you are a failure at meeting God's standards? Thank God that He has made another arrangement!

There is nothing that makes a greater hypocrite out of a person than for him to say, "I keep the Law!" No one can measure up to God's standards. Look at Israel. God is going to give them the Law and they say, "Bring it on, we are ready to keep it." What a display of self-confidence and arrogance. Yet there are multitudes of men and women today that claim they keep the Law even after God clearly demonstrated that no one can be saved by the Law—because no one can keep the Law. It was tried out under ideal conditions by the nation Israel.

ISRAEL PREPARES FOR A VISITATION BY GOD

And the Lord said unto Moses, Lo, I come unto thee in a thick cloud, that the people may hear when I speak with thee, and believe thee for ever. And Moses told the words of the people unto the Lord [Exod. 19:9].

There are some people who think that the giving of the Law was a beautiful event. Years ago a very cultured and refined southern lady said to me, "Mr. McGee, don't you think the giving of the Law was a beautiful, lovely thing?" I think I shocked her when I replied, "I do not see anything beautiful in it. It was a frightful and terrifying thing!"

> And the Lord said unto Moses, Go unto the people, and sanctify them to-day and to-morrow, and let them wash their clothes.

> And be ready against the third day: for the third day the Lord will come down in the sight of all the people upon mount Sinai [Exod. 19:10–11].

What a tremendous scene, but listen to what followed:

> And thou shalt set bounds unto the people round about, saying, Take heed to yourselves, that ye go not up into the mount, or touch the border of it: whosoever toucheth the mount shall be surely put to death [Exod. 19:12].

Does this sound like a beautiful scene? The children of Israel were told not to get near the mount and not to touch it or they would die. That, friends, is not beautiful; it is dreadful!

> There shall not an hand touch it, but he shall surely be stoned, or shot through; whether it be beast or man, it shall not live: when the trumpet soundeth long, they shall come up to the mount.

> And Moses went down from the mount unto the people, and sanctified the people; and they washed their clothes.

And he said unto the people, Be ready against the third day: come not at your wives.

And it came to pass on the third day in the morning, that there were thunders and lightnings, and a thick cloud upon the mount, and the voice of the trumpet exceeding loud; so that all the people that was in the camp trembled [Exod. 19:13-16].

This is not a circus parade going by, but this is the giving of God's Law. It was a terrifying experience and the people trembled because it was frightening.

And Moses brought forth the people out of the camp to meet with God; and they stood at the nether part of the mount.

And mount Sinai was altogether on a smoke, because the Lord descended upon it in fire: and the smoke therof ascended as the smoke of a furnace, and the whole mount quaked greatly.

And when the voice of the trumpet sounded long, and waxed louder and louder, Moses spake, and God answered him by a voice.

And the Lord came down upon mount Sinai, on the top of the mount: and the Lord called Moses up to the top of the mount; and Moses went up.

And the Lord said unto Moses, Go down, charge the people, lest they break through unto the Lord to gaze, and many of them perish [Exod. 19:17-21].

Some of the Israelites think they might see something spectacular, but they will not see anything. They will only hear a voice and it is still true to this day that "No man hath seen God at any time; the only begotten Son, which is in the bosom of the Father, he hath declared him" (John 1:18).

> And let the priests also, which come near to the LORD, sanctify themselves, lest the LORD break forth upon them.
>
> And Moses said unto the LORD, The people cannot come up to mount Sinai: for thou chargedst us, saying, Set bounds about the mount, and sanctify it.
>
> And the LORD said unto him, Away, get thee down, and thou shalt come up, thou, and Aaron with thee: but let not the priests and the people break through to come up unto the LORD, lest he break forth upon them.
>
> So Moses went down unto the people, and spake unto them [Exod. 19:22–25].

Israel's pledge to keep the Law was a mistake they never would have made had they known more about themselves and how weak they were. There is a great contrast between that dispensation of law and our dispensation of grace.

CHAPTER 20

THEME: The giving of the Ten Commandments; the
effect of God's visit; instructions concerning the altar

In chapter 20 of Exodus we have the giving of the Law. The Ten Commandments are given first but they are only part of the Law. Instructions pertaining to the altar are also given; the Law and the altar go
together. The Law revealed that man is a sinner and needs a Savior.
There must be an altar upon which to offer the sacrifice; there must
be the shedding of blood for sin. You have a mirror in your bathroom,
which is a picture of the Law, and there is a basin underneath the
mirror. You do not wash yourself with the mirror; it only reveals the
dirt. Just so, the Law is the mirror that reveals our sin. And beneath
that mirror there is a wash basin.

> There is a fountain filled with blood
> Drawn from Immanuel's veins,
> And sinners plunged beneath *that* flood,
> Lose all their guilty stains.

THE GIVING OF THE TEN COMMANDMENTS

The first part of the Law given to Israel was the Ten Commandments
which was a moral code.

And God spake all these words, saying,

**I am the Lord thy God, which have brought thee out of
the land of Egypt, out of the house of bondage [Exod.
20:1–2].**

God says, "I brought you out of Egypt and the house of bondage, and
upon that basis I want to give you My law." Israel asked for the Law

and God obliged them and He gave them the Ten Commandments first.

Several things need to be mentioned as we look at the Ten Commandments. The first one is the "new morality." The new morality goes back before the giving of the Law. In fact, it came right out of the Garden of Eden when man first disobeyed God. The new morality existed before the Flood and after the Flood. Today it is far from new. We love to think that we are sophisticated and refined sinners. We are not—we are just crude sinners in the raw—natural sinners. The Ten Commandments put before us God's standards. No man can play fast and loose with the Ten Commandments and get by with it.

On Blackwell's Island there was a graveyard for criminals. On one grave was a marker which read, "Here lies the fragments of John Smith who contradicted His Maker, played football with the Ten Commandments, and departed this life at the age of thirty-five. His mother and wife weep for him. Nobody else does. May he rest in peace." That grave marker revealed a man who tried to defy the law of God. No person can play football with the Ten Commandments and escape the punishment of God.

Often times the charge is made against those of us who preach the grace of God that we do not have a proper appreciation for the Law. We are charged with despising it, rejecting it, and actually teaching that because we are not saved by the Law, it can be violated at will and broken with impunity. This is not true at all. On the contrary, every preacher who teaches the grace of God and has a true perspective of the nature of salvation by faith, realizes the lofty character of the Law. Paul answers the problem in Romans 6:1-2 which says, "What shall we say then? Shall we continue in sin, that grace may abound? God forbid. How shall we, that are dead to sin, live any longer therein?"

If you think you can continue to live in sin and break the Ten Commandments at will, then, my friend, you are not saved by the grace of God. When you are really saved, you want to please God and want to do His will which is revealed in the Ten Commandments. Therefore I think every preacher of the grace of God has a respect and reverence for God's Law. We say with the psalmist, "O how love I thy law! it is my meditation all the day."

What is the Law? Someone has defined it as the transcript of the mind of God. That is a defective definition. The Law is the expression of the mind of God relative to what man ought to be. There is no grace or mercy in the Law at all. The Law is an expression of the holy will of God. The psalmist in Psalm 19:7 says, "The law of the LORD is perfect, converting the soul: the testimony of the LORD is sure, making wise the simple." The Law requires perfection on your part. I have never met anyone who has measured up to God's standard. The Law is not some vague notion, and it does not have anything to do with good intentions. It requires perfect obedience, for the Law of the Lord is perfect.

The Law of the Lord is right. Our notions of right and wrong are colored by our environment and by the fact that we have a fallen nature. The Law is a revelation of God. God has drawn the line between right and wrong. How do you know what is right? God tells us what is right. This present generation who wants freedom so badly is questioning what is right. "Why is it wrong to steal?" they ask. They do not mind stealing. But they like the commandment "Thou shalt not kill" because they say it is wrong for the government to commit murder by executing criminals. How inconsistent this crowd is! How ignorant they are of the Law. Why is it wrong to lie or to steal? Because God says it is wrong. You may say, "It is for the good of mankind." Of course it is. The Law would be a wonderful thing if man could keep it. Man cannot keep the Law, however, and the jails, the locks on the doors, and the fact that you have to sign ten pieces of paper to borrow money from a bank because they do not trust you, are all testimony to this fact. There was a day when a man's word was his bond, but that is no longer true today. The Law is a norm for human conduct. Stealing, lying, and adultery are wrong because God says they are wrong.

The Law never enforces itself. The Law-giver must have power. God enforces His laws with a tremendous impact. Take the law of gravitation, for example. You can go up as high as you want to but you had better not turn loose. The law of gravitation is in operation and you cannot reverse it. You may think you can, but in the long run you will be the loser.

Many people think they can break the Ten Commandments right

and left and get by with it. That reminds me of the whimsical story of the man who jumped off the Empire State Building in New York City. As he went sailing by the fiftieth floor, a man looked out the window and said to him, "Well, how is it?" The falling man replied, "So far, so good." That is not where the law of gravitation enforces itself. Fifty more floors down and the man will find out, "So far, *not* so good." The interesting thing is that a law must be enforced to be a law and therefore God says in Ezekiel 18:4, ". . . the soul that sinneth, it shall die." The Law must be enforced and the breaker of the Law must pay the penalty.

There is another viewpoint that needs to be corrected and that is the confounding of law and grace and putting them into one system. Putting law and grace into the same system is to rob the Law of its majesty and meaning. There is no love in the Law. There is no grace in the Law. Grace is robbed of its goodness and glory when it is mixed with the Law. Grace is stripped of its wonder, attractiveness, and desire. The sinner's needs are not met when law and grace are bound together. The Law sets forth what man ought to be. Grace sets forth what God is. The majesty of the Law is something that we do need to recognize.

The Law reveals who God is and the vast yawning chasm between God and man. Paul asked the question in Galatians 4:21, "Tell me, ye that desire to be under the law, do ye not hear the law?" You had better listen to what the Law says because man has been weighed in the balances by the Ten Commandments and has been found wanting. You do not measure yourself by others. It is very easy for the man on Mt. Whitney to look down at the man on the ant hill and say, "I am higher than you are." The man on Mt. Whitney, however, did not make it to the moon, or to heaven either. You just do not measure up to God's standard.

The Law also reveals who man is and his inability to bridge the gap between himself and God. Romans 3:19 tells us, "Now we know that what things soever the law saith, it saith to them who are under the law: that every mouth may be stopped, and all the world may become guilty before God." Paul says in Romans 8:3, "For what the law could not do, in that it was weak through the flesh, God sending his own Son in the likeness of sinful flesh, and for sin, condemned sin in the flesh." The fault does not lie in the Law but in us.

The Law is a mirror, as we have already seen, that reveals man in his sinful condition. Many people look in the mirror and think they are all right. This reminds me of the fairy story in which a queen looked in her mirror and said, "Mirror, mirror, on the wall, who is fairest of them all?" She wanted the mirror to say that she was, but the mirror told the truth and said she wasn't—someone else was fairer. And the interesting thing today is that a great many folk look at the mirror (the Ten Commandments in the Word of God) and they say the same thing, "Mirror, mirror on the wall, who is fairest of them all?" The difference is that they answer their own question and say, "I am." They think they are keeping the Law. My friend, you need to look in the mirror more closely and let the mirror do the answering.

The Law never made a man a sinner; it revealed the fact that man was a sinner. The Law was given to bring a man to Christ, as we have seen. It was our schoolmaster to take us by the hand, lead us to the Cross, and tell us, "Little man, you need a Savior because you are a sinner."

THE TEN COMMANDMENTS

Now let's look at the Ten Commandments. They are divided into two different major divisions. One part deals with man's relationship to God, and the other part deals with man's relationship to man.

Thou shalt have no other gods before me [Exod. 20:3].

God is condemning polytheism, which is the belief in more than one god. There is no commandment against atheism—there was none in those days because they were too close to the creation and the original revelation of God. The atheists began to appear during the time of King David, and they were called fools. Psalm 53:1 says, "The fool hath said in his heart, There is no God. . . ." Today the atheist can be a college professor and considered to be a brain and an intellectual, but God says he is a fool. There are many atheists today because we are so

far from our origin, and men are not willing to accept the revelation of
God in His Word.

God told Israel, "Thou shalt have no other gods before me." God
instructed the nation in this manner because in that day it was mighty
hard for man to keep balanced. In that day it was popular to worship
many gods. Today it is popular not to worship any god. My, how the
pendulum of the clock has moved! The important thing to note in this
verse is the fact that God is condemning polytheism. Paul elaborates
upon this subject in Romans 1:21–25 which states, "Because that,
when they knew God, they glorified him not as God, neither were
thankful; but became vain in their imaginations, and their foolish
heart was darkened. Professing themselves to be wise, they became
fools, And changed the glory of the uncorruptible God into an image
made like to corruptible man, and to birds, and fourfooted beasts, and
creeping things. Wherefore God also gave them up to uncleanness
through the lusts of their own hearts, to dishonour their own bodies
between themselves: Who changed the truth of God into a lie, and
worshipped and served the creature more than the Creator, who is
blessed for ever. Amen."

> **Thou shalt not make unto thee any graven image, or any
> likeness of any thing that is in heaven above, or that is in
> the earth beneath, or that is in the water under the
> earth:**
>
> **Thou shalt not bow down thyself to them, nor serve
> them: for I the LORD thy God am a jealous God, visiting
> the iniquity of the fathers upon the children unto the
> third and fourth generation of them that hate me [Exod.
> 20:4–5].**

Some people may feel that this passage does not apply to us today.
Colossians 3:5 tells us that ". . . covetousness . . . is idolatry." Anything that you give yourself to, especially in abandonment, becomes
your "god." Many people do not worship Bacchus, the cloven-footed
Greek and Roman god of wine and revelry of long ago, but they wor-

ship the bottle just the same. There are millions of alcoholics in our country right now. The liquor interests like to tell us about how much of the tax burden they carry, when actually they do not pay a fraction of the bill for the casualties they cause by their product. A lot of propaganda is being fed to this generation and large groups of people are being brainwashed. Whether or not folk recognize it, they worship the god Bacchus.

Other people worship Aphrodite, that is, the goddess of sex. Some people worship money. Anything to which you give your time, heart, and soul, becomes your god. God says that we are not to have any gods before Him.

Thou shalt not take the name of the LORD thy God in vain; for the LORD will not hold him guiltless that taketh his name in vain [Exod. 20:7].

Using the Lord's name in "vain" means in the way of blasphemy. This is very prevalent in our day and age. But His commandment still stands. It is wrong to use God's name in vain because He is God and He is holy! It also reveals a lack of vocabulary. Many people cannot express themselves without using profanity. A man who was wonderfully converted several years ago in Texas once told me, "When I was converted, I lost over half of my vocabulary!" And this is what he meant.

Now the fourth commandment:

Remember the sabbath day, to keep it holy.

Six days shalt thou labour, and do all thy work:

But the seventh day is the sabbath of the LORD thy God: in it thou shalt not do any work, thou, nor thy son, nor thy daughter, thy manservant, nor thy maidservant, nor thy cattle, nor thy stranger that is within thy gates:

For in six days the LORD made heaven and earth, the sea, and all that in them is, and rested the seventh day:

wherefore the LORD blessed the sabbath day, and hallowed it [Exod. 20:8–11].

The Sabbath Day was given to the nation Israel in a very unusual way. It was a covenant, a token between God and the children of Israel. We shall see that in Exodus 31:13–17. The exact day, in my opinion, is not important. After all, the calendar changes that have been made make it impossible for us to know whether our seventh day is our Saturday or not. I do not think it is. But that is beside the point because, as far as we are concerned, it makes no difference what day we observe. We keep what we believe is the first day of the week. It may or may not be. But we recognize the first day of our week because our LORD came back from the dead on that day. All of this will be dealt with later on in the Book of Exodus.

Next we come to the section of the commandments which deals with man's relationship with man. It begins in the home.

Honour thy father and thy mother: that thy days may be long upon the land which the LORD thy God giveth thee [Exod. 20:12].

A father and a mother should be worthy of the honor of their children. We will speak more of this commandment later.

The sixth commandment says:

Thou shalt not kill [Exod. 20:13].

This verse is used by many people who are opposed to a particular war. Many young men have talked to me about it. They say, "You should not kill; therefore, you should not be a soldier." The commandment "Thou shalt not kill" was *not* given to a nation; it was given to the individual. One man should not kill another. No one should go to any country on his own, and kill. "Thou shalt not kill" has nothing to do with soldier service or with the execution of a criminal. A nation is given an authority to protect human life by taking human life. "Thou shalt not kill" is a commandment to the individual and it is speaking of murder, which our LORD said comes from anger—and we are not even to be angry with our brother.

The seventh commandment says:

Thou shalt not commit adultery [Exod. 20:14].

We are living today in the middle of a sex revolution. Sex is certainly not new, but it is still adultery when it is committed outside of wedlock. God makes this very clear. Man may think he has changed this commandment but he has not. This commandment still stands.

The eighth commandment says:

Thou shalt not steal [Exod. 20:15].

The point I would like to make here is that if you are permitted to commit adultery, then you should be permitted to steal and so forth. This whole package goes together. If one is all right to indulge in, then all should be right; if one is wrong, then all are wrong.

The ninth commandment says:

Thou shalt not bear false witness against thy neighbour [Exod. 20:16].

Bearing false witness against your neighbor is lying.

The tenth commandment says:

Thou shalt not covet thy neighbour's house, thou shalt not covet thy neighbour's wife, nor his manservant, nor his maidservant, nor his ox, nor his ass, nor any thing that is thy neighbour's [Exod. 20:17].

Covetousness, according to the apostle Paul in Colossians 3:5, is idolatry. This is one of the great sins of the present hour. God condemns killing, adultery, stealing, bearing false witness, and covetousness.

We will have an occasion to look at the Ten Commandments in a different way later on.

THE EFFECT OF GOD'S VISIT

God has given the children of Israel the moral code which is the Ten Commandments. However, there is more to the Law than the moral code. God will also give them that part of the Law which deals with social legislation. He will also give them instructions concerning an altar and the building of the tabernacle. The Book of Leviticus gives in detail the service of the tabernacle. It is all part of the Law. It all goes in one package.

> **And all the people saw the thunderings, and the lightnings, and the noise of the trumpet, and the mountain smoking: and when the people saw it, they removed, and stood afar off.**

> **And they said unto Moses, Speak thou with us, and we will hear: but let not God speak with us, lest we die [Exod. 20:18–19].**

When the Israelites saw the thunder and lightning, they were afraid and backed away from the mount.

> **And Moses said unto the people, Fear not: for God is come to prove you, and that his fear may be before your faces, that ye sin not [Exod. 20:20].**

The Law presented a very high standard. The Law of the Lord is perfect. It demands perfection. If you are trying to be saved by keeping the Law, you will have to be *perfect*. If you are not perfect, you cannot be saved by the Law. I thank God that under grace He can take a poor sinner like me and save me. Grace reveals something of the goodness and wonder of our God.

And the people stood afar off, and Moses drew near unto the thick darkness where God was.

And the LORD said unto Moses, Thus thou shalt say unto the children of Israel, Ye have seen that I have talked with you from heaven.

Ye shall not make with me gods of silver, neither shall ye make unto you gods of gold [Exod. 20:21-23].

It is important to see why God appears in just this way to the children of Israel. I think it is evident that God wants to impress upon them that He is the living God. Remember that they were reared in Egypt with idols all around them—and they were and are idolatrous, as we shall see. They are worshiping the creature rather than the Creator. God is moving closer to these people than He ever has before.

INSTRUCTIONS CONCERNING THE ALTAR

God has given Israel the Ten Commandments. Now along with the commandments God gives instructions for an altar. An altar is used for sacrifice. This altar speaks of the Cross of Christ and the blood that He shed. This altar is the one they built before the tabernacle was made. Apparently everywhere they journeyed they made one like this.

An altar of earth thou shalt make unto me, and shalt sacrifice thereon thy burnt offerings, and thy peace offerings, thy sheep, and thine oxen: in all places where I record my name I will come unto thee, and I will bless thee [Exod. 20:24].

There is no mention of presenting a sin offering on this altar. The peace offering reveals that man needs a sacrifice that will reconcile him to God, and that Christ did make peace by the blood of His Cross. The burnt offering speaks of who Christ is; it speaks of His worthiness and ability to save.

This altar was to be made of earth and was the place upon which the Israelites were to sacrifice burnt offerings and peace offerings. The sin and trespass offerings were given to Israel later.

And if thou wilt make me an altar of stone, thou shalt not build it of hewn stone: for if thou lift up thy tool upon it, thou hast polluted it [Exod. 20:25].

There is an important lesson in this verse. God wanted them to build a plain altar of stone with no engraving. Perhaps an engraver would want to make the altar appealing, attractive looking, and very beautiful. The moment a tool is put to stones, it is polluted. God rejects it. Today we have gone way past "engraving" in our churches. We have come to the place where we feel that everything connected with worship should be beautiful. We want soft music, dim lights, and beautiful colors. We want the sermon to be given in very low tones and in a dignified manner, as flowery as possible. Well, we've been through such a period. And we have found that liberalism has emptied our churches. There is nothing wrong with an attractive place to worship. I am for soft lights, beautiful music, and flowery speaking. But when any of these things obscures the message of the Cross and takes attention away from the Lord Jesus Christ who died on that Cross, then God is offended. God does not want this to happen.

When Paul went to the city of Corinth, you will recall, he found the Corinthians to be quite philosophical. Many of the heathen priests connected with the heathen religions tried to identify with all the sins of Corinth. When Paul arrived, these secondhand philosophers wanted to argue, discuss, and appear intellectual. These Corinthians were going in every direction. Paul had a similar experience in Athens. He tells these Corinthians, "For I determined not to know any thing among you, save Jesus Christ, and him crucified" (1 Cor. 2:2). Friends, if "Jesus Christ and him crucified" is left out of the message, I do not care how high the steeple is, how loud the church bell is, how beautiful the sanctuary is, how soft the music is, or how educated the preacher is—it is not a church and, as far as God is concerned, it is polluted.

Neither shalt thou go up by steps unto mine altar, that thy nakedness be not discovered thereon [Exod. 20:26].

Many people would like to build nice lovely steps up to the altar. That would be very convenient. In that day a man wore a kind of a skirt and to climb steps he would have to lift that skirt and his nakedness would be revealed. God says, "I do not want to see your nakedness." That which speaks of the flesh God cannot use.

Let me make this very personal. Anything that Vernon McGee does that is of the flesh, God hates and will not use. God does not want a display of the flesh in anything that has to do with His work. We need to guard against this type of thing. It disturbs me when people see only the preacher and do not see the One he is trying to present. I personally do not like anyone to tell me that I preached a beautiful sermon. The last thing I want to do is preach a beautiful sermon. I want to preach about a beautiful Savior and when people hear me preach, I want them to say, "Isn't Jesus wonderful!"

I have had very few real compliments since I have been a minister, but one I remember well. When I was a pastor as a student in Georgia, I used to preach in a church on the side of a red clay hill. One morning after the message everyone left but a country boy. He wore high yellow shoes that buttoned all the way, and he waited around, as timid as could be. Finally he came up to me with tears in his eyes. He took hold of my hand and said, "My, I did not know Jesus was so wonderful." He wanted to say something else but he was too choked with emotion; so he turned and walked out of the little church. That church today is in the middle of a city, but in those days it was in the middle of a cotton patch. I watched that country boy walk across the cotton patch, and said to myself, "Oh God, let me so preach that people will know that Jesus is wonderful." That was a compliment and I have not had many like it.

We do not need the display of the flesh in the ministry, in the pulpit, or in church work. We need to preach Jesus Christ and Him crucified.

CHAPTER 21

THEME: The law concerning master and servant relationships; the law concerning personal injuries

THE LAW CONCERNING MASTER AND SERVANT RELATIONSHIPS

In Exodus 21 we come to social legislation. This part of the Law is an important issue at this time because the Israelites had been slaves in Egypt.

> Now these are the judgments which thou shalt set before them.

> If thou buy an Hebrew servant, six years he shall serve: and in the seventh he shall go out free for nothing [Exod. 21:1–2].

These two verses clearly state that the Israelites could never permanently make one of their own brethren a slave.

> If he came in by himself, he shall go out by himself: if he were married, then his wife shall go out with him.

> If his master have given him a wife, and she have born him sons or daughters; the wife and her children shall be her master's, and he shall go out by himself.

> And if the servant shall plainly say, I love my master, my wife, and my children; I will not go out free:

> Then his master shall bring him unto the judges; he shall also bring him to the door, or unto the door post; and his master shall bore his ear through with an awl; and he shall serve him for ever [Exod. 21:3–6].

This remarkable law states that if a man is a slave, after seven years he can go free. If he was married when he became a slave, he can take his wife with him. If he married while a slave, that is, if he married a woman who was already a slave of his master, at the end of seven years he could go free, but his wife would still belong to the master. He could, however, if he loved his wife and master, decide to stay on his own free will. If he decides to stay, his master is to bore his earlobe through with an awl signifying that he will serve his master forever.

This is a beautiful picture of the Lord Jesus Christ. He came to this earth and took upon Himself our humanity. And we were all slaves of sin. He could have gone out free. He could have returned to heaven, to His position in the Godhead, without going through the doorway of death. He did not have to die upon the Cross. But He willingly came down to earth and took upon Himself our humanity. "And being found in fashion as a man, he humbled himself, and became obedient unto death, even the death of the cross" (Phil. 2:8).

Psalm 40:6–8 goes on to say, "Sacrifice and offering thou didst not desire; mine ears hast thou opened: burnt offering and sin offering hast thou not required. Then said I, Lo, I come: in the volume of the book it is written of me, I delight to do thy will, O my God: yea, thy law is within my heart." This passage refers to Christ, because Hebrews 10:5–9 tells us that it does. It was fulfilled when our Lord came to this earth. "Wherefore when he cometh into the world [speaking of Christ], he saith, Sacrifice and offering thou wouldest not, but a body hast thou prepared me [it was not only his ear that was "digged," or bored through with an awl, but God gave Him a body which He will have throughout eternity]: In burnt offerings and sacrifices for sin thou hast had no pleasure. Then said I, Lo, I come (in the volume of the book it is written of me) to do thy will, O God. Above when he said, Sacrifice and offering and burnt offerings and offering for sin thou wouldest not, neither hadst pleasure therein; which are offered by the law; Then said he, Lo, I come to do thy will, O God. He taketh away the first, that he may establish the second." Christ was "made like unto His brethren." He chose not to go out free without us. He could have left this earth without dying, but He said, "I love My

Bride. I love the sinner." So He became obedient unto death, even the
death of the Cross so that He could redeem us from the slavery of sin.
What a picture this is of Christ—placed right here after the giving of
the Ten Commandments.

THE LAW CONCERNING PERSONAL INJURIES

**He that smiteth a man, so that he die, shall be surely put
to death [Exod. 21:12].**

This verse is the basis for capital punishment. Some people believe
that "Thou shalt not kill" means that the government has no right to
exact a death penalty. However, God commanded the nation Israel to
put to death any murderer.

**And if a man lie not in wait, but God deliver him into his
hand; then I will appoint thee a place whither he shall
flee [Exod. 21:13].**

There were six cities of refuge placed throughout the land of Palestine.
These were set up in convenient locations so that one charged with
manslaughter could avail himself of the shelter they afforded until the
matter in which he was involved could be settled. We will speak more
of the cities of refuge later.

**But if a man come presumptuously upon his neighbour,
to slay him with guile; thou shalt take him from mine
altar, that he may die [Exod. 21:14].**

If a man commits a premeditated murder, that man is to be executed.
If a man kills someone in self-defense while trying to defend himself,
without premeditation, that man would not merit execution.

And he that smiteth his father, or his mother, shall be
surely put to death [Exod. 21:15].

This is God's protection for the home.

And he that stealeth a man, and selleth him, or if he be
found in his hand, he shall surely be put to death [Exod.
21:16].

God did not approve of slavery at all and, in fact, He condemned it. It
was a great system in that day, but God dealt with it.

And he that curseth his father, or his mother, shall
surely be put to death.

And if men strive together, and one smite another with a
stone, or with his fist, and he die not, but keepeth his
bed:

If he rise again, and walk abroad upon his staff, then
shall he that smote him be quit: only he shall pay for the
loss of his time, and shall cause him to be thoroughly
healed [Exod. 21:17–19].

In other words, the one who was responsible for the injury was to
reimburse the injured—both for his time and medical expenses.
    The above laws and the other laws presented in the rest of this
chapter are the basis of the laws of our land. They form the basic plat-
form of law and order that is necessary for a civilized nation to build
upon.
    Verses 24 and 25 sum it all up by saying:

Eye for eye, tooth for tooth, hand for hand, foot for foot.

Burning for burning, wound for wound, stripe for stripe
[Exod. 21:24–25].

In other words, these two verses state the law of reciprocity. Law must be enforced if there is to be law and order and protection for human life and property.

Thank God, we do not have to depend on keeping the Law for our salvation. There is One who is prepared to extend grace to us that we may be saved, even the Lord Jesus Christ.

CHAPTER 22

THEME: The law concerning property rights; the law concerning crimes against humanity

THE LAW CONCERNING PROPERTY RIGHTS

There are those who raise the question today, "What is right and what is wrong?" Some say that what is right and wrong is relative. A college professor, who claims to be an atheist, was discussing this with me. He maintained that right and wrong are relative, that what he would think is right and what I would think is right could be poles apart. Then he asked me, "On what do you base your dogmatic conclusions?" I said, "I base them on the Word of God." I went on to tell him that my nature was just like his nature, and that I would like to give in in certain places, and I would like to let the bars down here and there, but God has given me a standard to follow. The interesting thing is that God's standard has produced a society in which there has been a measure of law and justice.

The laws presented in chapters 21 to 24 deal with everyday nitty-gritty living. In some ways it is boring reading and similar to reading a lawbook. However, most of our laws are based upon these precepts. I am glad that the Word of God says, "Thou shalt not kill." It protects me and my family. I am happy the Bible says, "Thou shalt not steal." It protects what little property I have. These and the other laws are basic to having order in a society.

> **If a man shall steal an ox, or a sheep, and kill it, or sell it; he shall restore five oxen for an ox, and four sheep for a sheep [Exod. 22:1].**

I cannot tell you why *five* oxen should be restored for an ox or *four* sheep for one sheep. In the New Testament, however, Zacchaeus referred to this principle:"And Zacchaeus stood, and said unto the Lord; Behold, Lord, the half of my goods I give to the poor; and if I have taken any thing from any man by false accusation, I restore him *fourfold*" (Luke 19:8). Why did he say fourfold? He was referring to the Mosaic Law.

Our law today says that if you destroy another man's property, you must pay the damages. All that our society demands when you damage or destroy some other person's property is to replace the item or pay what it is worth. God's law of restoring fourfold is much better with human nature the way it is. If we had to restore fourfold anything that we destroyed or damaged, we would be more careful. Human nature is always the same, and God is always the same. God deals with man on the basis that is best for him.

If a thief be found breaking up, and be smitten that he die, there shall no blood be shed for him [Exod. 22:2].

This law gives you the right to self-protection. Not long ago a thief broke into a man's place and the homeowner shot him. He sued the homeowner for several thousand dollars in damages. The case went to court and the thief won the judgment on the grounds that the homeowner had no right to shoot him, according to the decision of some asinine judge! In order to pay the damages the homeowner had to sell his property. And there was no judgment against the thief at all! In our day there is a great emphasis on protecting the rights of the *guilty* at the expense of the rights of the *innocent*.

God's law protects a man's property and his home. Under this principle a man is justified in protecting his property, his home, and his loved ones.

God's laws are basic principles which give society law and order. If mankind had followed God's social legislation as given in the Book of Exodus, we would not have the social problems we are having in the cities of the United States. Our entire legal system, which was founded on the Word of God, is riddled with men who do not know the Bible because they are so far from it themselves. Their entire background is such that they are not properly able to interpret the Law.

The Constitution of the United States was written by men, not all of whom were Christian (in fact, most of them were Deists), but they had a certain respect for the Word of God. I recently heard a man say that Thomas Jefferson ridiculed the Bible. He did not. Quotations from Thomas Jefferson show that he had great respect for the Word of God even though he did not believe in the miraculous and actually did not follow it in his personal life. But we have men who administer law today with no background in the Bible whatever. Because of this we are in trouble, deep trouble.

If the sun be risen upon him, there shall be blood shed for him; for he should make full restitution; if he have nothing, then he shall be sold for his theft [Exod. 22:3].

If a man steals, he has to make restitution for that which he has stolen, even to the point of selling himself into slavery to help make the payment.

If a man shall cause a field or vineyard to be eaten, and shall put in his beast, and shall feed in another man's field; of the best of his own field, and of the best of his own vineyard, shall he make restitution [Exod. 22:5].

If a man's cow or sheep breaks through into another man's field and they cause damage, he is to make restitution.

If fire break out, and catch in thorns, so that the stacks of corn, or the standing corn, or the field, be consumed therewith; he that kindled the fire shall surely make restitution [Exod. 22:6].

This is a practical verse that shows us the right way to do things. It is another basic principle for the welfare of mankind on earth. God gave the Mosaic system to Israel so that they would be an example to the nations of the world.

THE LAW CONCERNING CRIMES
AGAINST HUMANITY

And if a man entice a maid that is not betrothed, and lie with her, he shall surely endow her to be his wife [Exod. 22:16].

In other words, if a man rapes a girl, he will be forced to marry her. Things are certainly different in our day and age.

If her father utterly refuse to give her unto him, he shall pay money according to the dowry of virgins [Exod. 22:17].

If her father does not agree to the marriage, the rapist must pay a penalty for what he has done.

Thou shalt not suffer a witch to live [Exod. 22:18].

Today we are seeing a resurgence of Satan worship and of the supernatural. This trend is potent and it is real. We shall be dealing with this further in the Book of Deuteronomy.

Whosoever lieth with a beast shall surely be put to death [Exod. 22:19].

Having sexual intercourse with a beast shows just how low man can go. Why did God make a law like this? Well, because it was being done. And we are seeing a recurrence of this unspeakably degrading practice in our "enlightened" society.

He that sacrificeth unto any god, save unto the Lord only, he shall be utterly destroyed [Exod. 22:20].

This, of course, was the most severe penalty. Had it been followed to the letter, we would have a much better society today. Utterly destroying anyone who sacrifices to any other god but the LORD is harsh but, after all, when you have a cancer, you want to rid yourself of it. This is what God is talking about.

Thou shalt neither vex a stranger, nor oppress him: for ye were strangers in the land of Egypt [Exod. 22:21].

This is God's "Good Neighbor" policy.

Ye shall not afflict any widow, or fatherless child [Exod. 22:22].

Child labor laws were established after the Wesleyan Revival, friends. The Word of God has been basic to all of the great movements that have brought blessing to mankind. What about the fatherless child? Did the orphans' home begin in atheistic countries or under Christian auspices?

If thou afflict them in any wise, and they cry at all unto me, I will surely hear their cry:

And my wrath shall wax hot, and I will kill you with the sword; and your wives shall be widows, and your children fatherless [Exod. 22:23–24].

I believe that God protects the helpless. Great judgment is coming for those individuals who have mistreated folk in need.

If thou lend money to any of my people that is poor by thee, thou shalt not be to him as an usurer, neither shalt thou lay upon him usury [Exod. 22:25].

If one person lends money to another, he is not to charge excessive interest. God says it is wrong to take advantage of others.

These are some of God's laws, and more are given in Exodus 23.

CHAPTER 23

THEME: The law concerning property rights—
continued; the law concerning the land and the
Sabbath; the law concerning national feasts

THE LAW CONCERNING PROPERTY
RIGHTS—CONTINUED

**Thou shalt not raise a false report: put not thine hand
with the wicked to be an unrighteous witness [Exod.
23:1].**

Be careful what you say; this is God's rule of conduct. A gossiper is
as bad as a murderer, a thief, or an adulterer in your midst, yet in
our society a gossiper gets by easily.

**Thou shalt not follow a multitude to do evil; neither
shalt thou speak in a cause to decline after many to
wrest judgment [Exod. 23:2].**

If we were to follow God's precept, "Thou shalt not follow a multitude
to do evil," it would put us out of the marching, protesting and rioting
business. Also it would rid our society of the growing menace of
gangs. I talked with a very attractive young fellow in this category. He
said he dressed as he did because he wanted liberty and freedom. I
noticed there were several thousand dressed just like him. So I asked
him, "Would you dare dress differently? Would they accept you?" He
said, "No." Then I said, "When they protest, you have to get in line
and protest, don't you?" He said, "Yes, I do." "Well," I replied, "then
you really do not have much freedom, do you? You have to do certain
things. When they dress a certain way, you have to dress a certain way.
This is not freedom." My friend, freedom is not following a multitude
to do evil!

Neither shalt thou countenance a poor man in his cause
[Exod. 23:3].

Judgment should not be swayed toward the rich or toward the poor.
Judgment and justice should be exercised fairly. The Romans depic-
ted justice as a woman, tender but also blindfolded. She was no re-
specter of persons and held a sword in one hand and scales in the
other. The sword meant that when the judgment was handed down,
there would be the execution of the penalty. The scales meant that
justice would be fair. Judgment should be exercised without respect of
persons.

THE LAW CONCERNING THE LAND
AND THE SABBATH

Once again God gives Israel this law concerning the Sabbath Day
and the Sabbatic Year.

And six years thou shalt sow thy land, and shalt gather
in the fruits thereof:

But the seventh year thou shalt let it rest and lie still;
that the poor of thy people may eat: and what they leave
the beasts of the field shall eat. In like manner thou
shalt deal with thy vineyard, and with thy oliveyard
[Exod. 23:10–11].

God will review this law with Israel when they go into the land. The
subjects of the Sabbath Day, the Sabbatic Year, and the year of Jubilee
are dealt with in the Book of Leviticus. Briefly, the Sabbath Day was
the seventh day of the week and was a day of strict rest. The Sabbatic
Year was the septennial rest for the land from all cultivation. The year
of Jubilee is also called the year of liberty. Every fiftieth year the Hebrews who had been forced to sell themselves into slavery became
free. Lands that had been sold reverted to their original owners.

It is interesting to note that folk today who claim to be Sabbath keepers, are attempting to keep only the Sabbath *Day*. They ignore the Sabbath Year (especially if they are farmers) and disregard completely the year of Jubilee.

THE LAW CONCERNING NATIONAL FEASTS

Three times thou shalt keep a feast unto me in the year.

Thou shalt keep the feast of unleavened bread: (thou shalt eat unleavened bread seven days, as I commanded thee, in the time appointed of the month Abib; for in it thou camest out from Egypt: and none shall appear before me empty:)

And the feast of harvest, the firstfruits of thy labours, which thou hast sown in the field: and the feast of ingathering, which is in the end of the year, when thou hast gathered in thy labours out of the field.

Three times in the year all thy males shall appear before the Lord GOD [Exod. 23:14–17].

Three times a year all the Hebrew males were to appear before the Lord God in Jerusalem. There were three feasts that were to be celebrated: (1) the Feast of the Passover; (2) the Feast of Pentecost; (3) the Feast of Tabernacles. The Feast of the Passover, you will recall, was instituted in memory of Israel's preservation from the last plague brought against the land of Egypt and her deliverance from that land of bondage. Before the people of Israel enter the Promised Land, these will be discussed in detail.

Behold, I send an Angel before thee, to keep thee in the way, and to bring thee into the place which I have prepared.

Beware of him, and obey his voice, provoke him not; for he will not pardon your transgressions: for my name is in him [Exod. 23:20–21].

Who is this Angel? Other Scriptures shed light on the answer. First Corinthians 10:4 says, "And did all drink the same spiritual drink: for they drank of that spiritual Rock that followed them: and that Rock was Christ." First Corinthians 10:9–10 continues, "Neither let us tempt Christ, as some of them also tempted, and were destroyed of serpents. Neither murmur ye, as some of them also murmured, and were destroyed of the destroyer." It is the Lord Jesus that they were to obey. He is definitely the one in view here.

For mine Angel shall go before thee, and bring thee in unto the Amorites, and the Hittites, and the Perizzites, and the Canaanites, the Hivites, and the Jebusites: and I will cut them off [Exod. 23:23].

God told Israel that He intended to put the enemy out of the land because of their sin. Now the Lord says to them:

I will send my fear before thee, and will destroy all the people to whom thou shalt come, and I will make all thine enemies turn their backs unto thee [Exod. 23:27].

God is telling Israel that it is His intention to put them in the land of Israel and make it their land. Then God tells them:

Thou shalt make no covenant with them, nor with their gods.

They shall not dwell in thy land, lest they make thee sin against me: for if thou serve their gods, it will surely be a snare unto thee [Exod. 23:32–33].

The children of Israel were not to make any covenants with the inhabitants of the land nor with their gods. Joshua made the mistake of making a covenant with the Gibeonites. He did not do enough investigating. Of course the reason the nation of Israel finally went into Babylonian captivity was because they went into idolatry and served other gods. In other words, they did not heed God's warning.

CHAPTER 24

THEME: Order of worship before the existence of the tabernacle; the children of Israel acknowledge the covenant; Moses ascends Mount Sinai alone

Exodus 24 concludes the section on social legislation begun in Exodus 21. We have found that the Law of Moses is much more than the brief Ten Commandments and that the area of social legislation covers a great deal of ground.

ORDER OF WORSHIP BEFORE THE EXISTENCE OF THE TABERNACLE

And he said unto Moses, Come up unto the LORD, thou, and Aaron, Nadab, and Abihu, and seventy of the elders of Israel; and worship ye afar off [Exod. 24:1].

God told these men to come up into the mountain, but even these men who were in a very unique position at that time were told to *worship afar off.* How different things were under law than they are under grace. How different their situation was from when God was bringing them along the path from Egypt on eagles' wings of grace. Under law man must worship afar off but today Ephesians 2:13 tells us, "But now in Christ Jesus ye who sometimes were far off are made nigh by the blood of Christ." God saves us and leads us along life's pathway today by His grace.

And Moses alone shall come near the LORD: but they shall not come nigh; neither shall the people go up with him.

And Moses came and told the people all the words of the LORD, and all the judgments: and all the people an-

swered with one voice, and said, All the words which
the Lord hath said will we do [Exod. 24:2-3].

This is the second time that the children of Israel have given an affir-
mative answer when God asked them if they wanted His commandments and Law. They are very self-confident, self-sufficient, and
almost arrogant when they tell God, "Yes, we want your Law." They
promise to do all of the words of the Lord even before they have them
all. They have been given the Ten Commandments and believe they
can keep them.

One wonders how Israel could be so deceived. But I am even more
puzzled by the many people who still believe they are living by the
Law. Those who believe they are meeting God's standard are deceived, and it is a terrible thing. First John 1:8 tells us: "If we say that
we have no sin, we deceive ourselves, and the truth is not in us." You
won't be deceiving your neighbors, you will not deceive your wife
nor husband nor loved ones, but you certainly can deceive yourself. If
you say that you do not sin, you deceive yourself. You would think
that a man who says he has no sin ought to have also a little truth in
him. But John says there is no truth in him at all. In case you missed
it, John repeats it in 1 John 1:10, which says, "If we say that we have
not sinned, we make him a liar, and his word is not in us." He said that
if you say that you have not sinned, you have made God a liar. Friends,
God is no liar. I wouldn't call Him that if I were you. The best thing to
do is not boast of your goodness. My, the arrogance of the children of
Israel in saying, "All the words which the Lord hath said we will do!"
You will notice, however, that they did not keep all His words.

THE CHILDREN OF ISRAEL
ACKNOWLEDGE THE COVENANT

And Moses wrote all the words of the Lord, and rose up
early in the morning, and builded an altar under the
hill, and twelve pillars, according to the twelve tribes of
Israel.

> And he sent young men of the children of Israel, which
> offered burnt offerings, and sacrificed peace offerings of
> oxen unto the LORD.
>
> And Moses took half of the blood, and put it in basins;
> and half of the blood he sprinkled on the altar.
>
> And he took the book of the covenant, and read in the
> audience of the people: and they said, All that the LORD
> hath said will we do, and be obedient [Exod. 24:4–7].

These Israelites were certainly confident. In fact, they were filled with self-confidence. They really thought they could keep God's Law, and that is the worst kind of self-deception. They promised to obey God, but they did not. The natural man believes he can please God, but he cannot. You and I cannot please God because no man can meet God's standard. We forget that we are actually members of a totally depraved race as far as God is concerned. If you doubt it, just look around the world and note the lawlessness. Look at the sin, the confusion, the atheism, and the godlessness on every hand. God is absolutely right when He says in Romans 3:10, ". . . There is none righteous, no, not one." We live in a day when sin is called good and bad is called good. The prophets said that such a day would come. Well, we certainly have arrived.

> And Moses took the blood, and sprinkled it on the peo-
> ple, and said, Behold the blood of the covenant, which
> the LORD hath made with you concerning all these words
> [Exod. 24:8].

Even before God gives the Law to them, the Israelites are sprinkled with blood to let them know that there must be a sacrifice. Hebrews 9:22 says, "And almost all things are by the law purged with blood; and without shedding of blood is no remission." God will repeat this many times. Life must be given up, and a penalty must be paid before any of us can go to heaven.

MOSES ASCENDS MOUNT SINAI ALONE

Then went up Moses, and Aaron, Nadab, and Abihu, and seventy of the elders of Israel:

And they saw the God of Israel: and there was under his feet as it were a paved work of a sapphire stone, and as it were the body of heaven in his clearness [Exod. 24:9–10].

"They *saw* the God of Israel" needs to be understood in the light of other Scriptures. Actually no one has seen God because He is a Spirit. John 1:18 tells us that, "No man hath seen God at any time; the only begotten Son, which is in the bosom of the Father, he hath declared him." What they saw was a representation of God. I sincerely doubt that we shall see God the Father throughout eternity. Jesus Christ is probably the closest view we will have of the Father. But He will be enough to satisfy our hearts. All that we know today about the Father is through the Son. I do not know how God the Father looks, or feels, or thinks, because God has told us in Isaiah 55:8–9, "For my thoughts are not your thoughts, neither are your ways my ways, saith the LORD. For as the heavens are higher than the earth, so are my ways higher than your ways, and my thoughts than your thoughts." But Jesus has revealed Him to us. Moses, Aaron, Nadab, Abihu, and the seventy elders of Israel did not see God the Father but they saw a representation of God.

And upon the nobles of the children of Israel he laid not his hand: also they saw God, and did eat and drink [Exod. 24:11].

In this verse, as in the previous one, they saw a representation of God. Later on Moses asks to see God because all he had seen was a representation. Moses wanted to *see* God. Also to see God was Philip's plea in the upper room. "Philip saith unto him, Lord, shew us the Father, and it sufficeth us. Jesus saith unto him, Have I been so long time with you, and yet hast thou not known me, Philip? he that hath seen me hath seen the Father; and how sayest thou then, Shew us the Father?" (John 14:8–9). If you want to see God, friends, you will have to go through Jesus Christ.

I have heard earnest laymen give testimony to the fact that they can come directly into the presence of God since their salvation. The truth is that we do not come directly into God's presence; we have a mediator. "For there is one God, and one mediator between God and men, the man Christ Jesus" (1 Tim. 2:5). You come to God through Christ Jesus the mediator. Christ is the *daysman* Job longed for. Christ puts one hand in the Father's hand and one in your hand and brings you and God together. We do not reach God the Father on our own, and we must recognize that.

> **And Moses rose up, and his minister Joshua: and Moses went up into the mount of God [Exod. 24:13].**

Now Joshua is beginning to appear in the picture more. God is preparing him to succeed Moses. He is a young man, and God has many things to teach him before he is prepared to lead Israel.

> **And he said unto the elders, Tarry ye here for us, until we come again unto you: and, behold, Aaron and Hur are with you: if any man have any matters to do, let him come unto them.**
>
> **And Moses went up into the mount, and a cloud covered the mount.**
>
> **And the glory of the LORD abode upon mount Sinai, and the cloud covered it six days: and the seventh day he called unto Moses out of the midst of the cloud.**
>
> **And the sight of the glory of the LORD was like devouring fire on the top of the mount in the eyes of the children of Israel.**

And Moses went into the midst of the cloud, and gat him up into the mount: and Moses was in the mount forty days and forty nights [Exod. 24:14–18].

It was during this time on Mount Sinai that Moses received the instructions presented in the rest of this book.

CHAPTER 25

THEME: Materials to be used for the tabernacle; instructions for constructing the ark of the covenant; the table of showbread; the golden lampstand

In chapters 25 through 30 of Exodus, God gives Israel the blueprint for the tabernacle and the pattern for the garments for the high priest. Next we have the construction and erection of the tabernacle and the fact that it was filled with the glory of the Lord. The tabernacle was to be the center of Israel's life because it was there where man would approach God.

MATERIALS TO BE USED FOR THE TABERNACLE

And the Lord spake unto Moses, saying,

Speak unto the children of Israel, that they bring me an offering: of every man that giveth it willingly with his heart ye shall take my offering [Exod. 25:1–2].

Israel had been out of slavery for only a few months, yet the Lord asks them to make a contribution to help build the tabernacle. The amazing thing is that the children of Israel gave so much they were told to stop giving! Friends, a thing like this does not happen very often. I was a pastor for a long time, and I never had to restrain folk from giving to the church. But Moses did!

Following are the items they were to bring:

> **And this is the offering which ye shall take of them; gold, and silver, and brass,**
>
> **And blue, and purple, and scarlet, and fine linen, and goats' hair,**

And rams' skins dyed red, and badgers' skins, and shittim wood,

Oil for the light, spices for anointing oil, and for sweet incense,

Onyx stones, and stones to be set in the ephod, and in the breastplate [Exod. 25:3-7].

Our first reaction is, "Where did they obtain these items?" Remember that Israel had just been delivered out of slavery and this was part of the four hundred years back wages that they collected on their way out of the land of Egypt. Exodus 12:36 reminds us that ". . . the LORD gave the people favour in the sight of the Egyptians, so that they lent unto them such things as they required. And they spoiled the Egyptians." When Israel left Egypt, they took out tremendous wealth. It has been estimated that at least five million dollars worth of material went into the construction of the tabernacle alone. The tabernacle was small in size because it had to be carried on the wilderness march, but it was very ornate, rich, and beautiful.

And let them make me a sanctuary; that I may dwell among them [Exod. 25:8].

God never said that He was going to *live* in the tabernacle in the sense that He was restricted to a geographical spot. He did say, however, that He would *dwell* between the cherubim. 1 Samuel 4:4, 2 Samuel 6:2, 2 Kings 19:15 and Isaiah 37:16 all give testimony to this fact. Israel was a theocracy and Jehovah was the King. Israel was to be ruled by God. His throne was between the cherubim, and this is where man met God. The idea which exists today that God dwells in a building made by hands is not true. That is a pagan notion. Some people call a church building "God's house." It is not God's house because He does not dwell in a building and never did. Solomon expressed it accurately, "But will God indeed dwell on the earth? behold, the heaven and heaven of heavens cannot contain thee; how much less this house

that I have builded?" (1 Kings 8:27). The tabernacle was to be the
place where man meets with God. "The LORD reigneth; let the people
tremble: he sitteth between the cherubims; let the earth be moved"
(Ps. 99:1). The ark was God's throne and it was the first article of furniture that they were to build.

> **According to all that I shew thee, after the pattern of the
> tabernacle, and the pattern of all the instruments
> thereof, even so shall ye make it [Exod. 25:9].**

The Book of Hebrews tells us that this earthly tabernacle was pat-
terned after the tabernacle in heaven. The question arises, "Is there a
literal tabernacle in heaven?" I take the position that there is because
God says there is. I take this literally and feel that if God had meant
something else, He would have made that clear also. Hebrews 8:5
says, "Who serve unto the example and shadow of heavenly things, as
Moses was admonished of God when he was about to make the tabernacle: for, See, saith he, that thou make all things according to the
pattern shewed to thee in the mount." Hebrews 9:23–24 goes on to say,
"It was therefore necessary that the patterns of things in the heavens
should be purified with these; but the heavenly things themselves
with better sacrifices than these. For Christ is not entered into the holy
places made with hands, which are the figures of the true; but into
heaven itself, now to appear in the presence of God for us."

INSTRUCTIONS FOR CONSTRUCTING
THE ARK OF THE COVENANT

The outer court was an enclosed place around the tabernacle proper,
100 cubits long by 50 cubits wide. The cubit was a unit of measure
based on the length of the forearm from the tip of the middle finger to
the elbow. If you measure yours, you will find it is about eighteen
inches—if you are a small person it will be shorter than that; if you are
tall, it will be longer. So the length of a cubit varied, but was about
eighteen inches. If you will consult the floor plan of the tabernacle,
you will see that in the outer court were the brazen altar and the laver

(Exod. 30:28). The tabernacle proper was divided into two compartments, the Holy Place and the Holy of Holies. The tabernacle itself was
thirty cubits long and ten cubits wide and ten cubits high. The Holy
Place was twenty by ten cubits. The Holy of Holies was ten cubits
long, ten cubits wide, and ten cubits high, thus making it a perfect
cube.

The furniture in the Holy Place consisted of the table of showbread, the golden lampstand, and the altar of incense. In the Holy of
Holies were the ark of the covenant and the mercy seat. In the outer
court were two articles of furniture: the brazen altar and the laver.
Enclosing it was a fence of white linen.

> **And they shall make an ark of shittim wood: two cubits
> and a half shall be the length thereof, and a cubit and a
> half the breadth thereof, and a cubit and a half the
> height thereof.**
>
> **And thou shalt overlay it with pure gold, within and
> without shalt thou overlay it, and shalt make upon it a
> crown of gold round about.**
>
> **And thou shalt cast four rings of gold for it, and put
> them in the four corners thereof; and two rings shall be
> in the one side of it, and two rings in the other side of it.**
>
> **And thou shalt make staves of shittim wood, and over-
> lay them with gold [Exod. 25:10–13].**

The ark and the mercy seat above it was the place where God would
meet with the children of Israel. It was the place for them to approach
their God. It was the sanctum sanctorum of the tabernacle. Notice that
the first article of furniture is the ark. We are approaching it from
God's viewpoint, from the inside looking out. The ark was in the Holy
of Holies where God's presence dwelt. If we were approaching it from
man's viewpoint, we would come first to the gate of the tabernacle,
then the brazen altar and the laver.

The tabernacle was fashioned in such a way that it could be carried

as the Israelites marched through the wilderness. It was put together
when they made camp and taken down when they moved to another
place. Each piece of furniture in the tabernacle was equipped with
rings and staves so that it could be easily carried through the wilderness.

The mercy seat, which formed a top for the ark, was considered a
separate piece of furniture.

> And thou shalt make a mercy seat of pure gold: two cu-
> bits and a half shall be the length thereof, and a cubit
> and a half the breadth thereof.
>
> And thou shalt make two cherubims of gold, of beaten
> work shalt thou make them, in the two ends of the mercy
> seat.
>
> And make one cherub on the one end, and the other
> cherub on the other end: even of the mercy seat shall ye
> make the cherubims on the two ends thereof [Exod.
> 25:17–19].

Notice what God now says:

> And the cherubims shall stretch forth their wings on
> high, covering the mercy seat with their wings, and
> their faces shall look one to another; toward the mercy
> seat shall the faces of the cherubims be [Exod. 25:20].

The cherubim looked down upon the mercy seat.

> And thou shalt put the mercy seat above upon the ark;
> and in the ark thou shalt put the testimony that I shall
> give thee.
>
> And there I will meet with thee, and I will commune
> with thee from above the mercy seat, from between the

two cherubims which are upon the ark of the testimony, of all things which I will give thee in commandment unto the children of Israel [Exod. 25:21–22].

The ark was a chest covered inside and outside with gold. It was made of shittim wood which was more or less indestructible and much like the redwood of California. It was a perfect symbol of the Lord Jesus Christ in His deity and humanity. Jesus Christ was the God-man; His deity was represented by the gold and His humanity was represented by the wood.

The ark could not be spoken of as merely a wooden chest because it also was a gold chest. It could not be called a golden chest because it was also a chest of wood. It required both gold and wood to maintain the symbolism pointing to Christ as the God-man. There is no mingling of the two. To overlook this duality is to entertain a monstrous notion of His person. There is no doctrine in Scripture so filled with infinite mystery and so removed from the realm of explanation as the hypostatical union of Christ, the God-man. Yet there is no symbol so simple as the ark that describes this union of God and man in one body. A mere box made of wood and gold speaks of things unfathomable. Truly God chooses the simple things to confound the wise. That simple box tells the whole story, as far as man can take it in, of the unsearchable mystery of the blessed person of the Lord Jesus Christ.

The ark was covered with gold both inside and outside. Colossians 2:9 tells us, "For in him dwelleth all the fulness of the Godhead bodily." Jesus Christ was not merely a thaumaturgist, that is, a wonder-worker. Nor was He a man with an overdeveloped God consciousness. He *was* God! He spoke as God. He put Himself on the same plane as God. In John 14:1, 9, our Savior says, "Let not your heart be troubled: ye believe in God, believe also in me. . . . Have I been so long time with you, and yet hast thou not known me, Philip? he that hath seen me hath seen the Father. . . ." Yes, He was God.

He was also perfectly man. He grew tired. He sat down to rest at a well in Samaria in the heat of the day. He slept, He ate, He drank, He laughed, He wept, and beyond all that, He suffered and died. All of these are human characteristics. The gold and the wood in the ark were both required, yet neither was mingled with the other. Nor was the identity of one lost in the other. Christ was both God and man, but the two natures were never fused or merged. He never functioned at the same time as both God and man. What He did was either perfectly human or perfectly divine.

The ark was not an empty box. It contained three items which are enumerated in Hebrews 9:4; "Which had the golden censer, and the ark of the covenant overlaid round about with gold, wherein was the golden pot that had manna, and Aaron's rod that budded, and the tables of the covenant." The contents of the ark were also symbolic. Aaron's rod that budded speaks of the Lord's resurrection. The manna speaks of the fact that Christ is the Bread of Life. The Ten Commandments speak of the life He lived on earth fulfilling the Law in all points and fulfilling the prophecies spoken of Him.

The tables of the covenant speak of the Kingship of Christ. He was born a King. He lived a King. He died a King, and He rose from the dead a King. He is coming again to earth as King. God's program is moving today and has been moving from eternity past to the time when Christ shall rule over this earth. Earth needs a ruler. Man needs a King. Someday He is coming as King of kings and Lord of lords.

The pot of manna speaks of Christ as a prophet. He spoke for God as John 6:32 clearly shows: ". . . Verily, verily, I say unto you, Moses gave you not that bread from heaven; but my Father giveth you the true bread from heaven." Jesus Christ was also God's message to man. He was to Logos, the Word of God, the very alphabet of God, the Alpha and Omega. He is God's final message to man. Since Christ came to earth as God-man, heaven has been silent because God has no addenda to place after Christ. He has no postscript to the letter because Christ is the embodiment of that letter. God told out His heart in Christ.

Aaron's rod that budded speaks of the work of Christ as priest. The prophet spoke for God before man; the priest spoke for man before God. As priest Christ offered Himself. As a priest He passed into heaven. Even now He sits at God's right hand in heaven. Jesus Christ the God-man was raised from the dead and He is the unique example of resurrection up to the present hour. Easter lilies and eggs do not speak of the resurrection, but Aaron's rod that budded does. It was an old dead stick that came alive. The ark speaks of Christ as prophet, priest, and king. "And the Word was made flesh, and dwelt among us, (and we beheld his glory, the glory as of the only begotten of the Father,) full of grace and truth" (John 1:14).

The mercy seat rested on top of the ark. It served as the top for the chest, the ark, but it was a separate piece of furniture. It was made of pure gold with cherubim on each end with their wings spread, over-shadowing it, and looking down upon the top where the blood was placed. It was here the high priest sprinkled the blood of the sacrifice. It was the blood that made it the mercy seat. This too was symbolic of the work of Christ. Christ literally presented His blood in heaven after His death on the Cross. A critic recommended my book, The Tabernacle, God's Portrait of Christ, but warned people that I took everything literally and must be watched carefully because I held the position that Christ offered His blood in heaven. The critic felt this was crude. I do not believe this is crude because the blood of Christ is not crude; it is precious. Peter calls his Savior's blood "precious" in 1 Peter 1:18–19, "Forasmuch as ye know that ye were not redeemed with corruptible things, as silver and gold, from your vain conversation received by tradition from your fathers; but with the precious blood of Christ, as of a lamb without blemish and without spot." Christ's blood is more precious than silver or gold. The most valuable thing in heaven is the blood He shed for man on earth. He presented His blood as He entered heaven and that is what makes God's throne a mercy seat for us today. We are bidden to come to God today on the basis of the fact that Jesus Christ, our great High Priest, has offered His own blood for our sins. Hebrews 4:14–16 reminds us that, "Seeing then that we have a great high priest, that is passed into the heavens, Jesus the Son of God, let us hold fast our profession. For we have not an high priest which cannot be touched with the feeling of our infirmities; but was in all points tempted like as we are, yet without sin. Let us therefore come boldly unto the throne of grace, that we may obtain mercy, and find grace to help in time of need."

You and I approach God through our great High Priest in heaven.

He is the living Christ at God's right hand. Through Him we find mercy and help. Many believers are trying to fight the battle down here alone. They are trying to meet the issues of life alone. Friends, you and I are not able to do it. We are not strong enough. We need help. And we are not availing ourselves to the help Christ offers. Paul prayed for the Ephesians that the mighty power that worked in Christ, bringing Him from the dead, might work in them (Eph. 1:19–20). We see very little of that power working in believers today. We need to lay hold of it by faith because we have a High Priest who is at God's right hand.

The high priest who served in this tabernacle rushed into the Holy Place, sprinkled the blood on the mercy seat, and rushed out again. Christ, our High Priest, when He made His offering, sat down at God's right hand and is still there for us today. He died down here to save us. He lives in heaven to keep us saved. And we should keep in contact with Him. Have you had a talk with Him today?

We have looked now at the articles of furniture in the Holy of Holies: the ark and the mercy seat. Now we will consider the furniture in the second compartment, the Holy Place.

THE TABLE OF SHOWBREAD

There are three articles of furniture in the Holy Place: (1) the golden lampstand, (2) the table of showbread, and (3) the altar of incense. Inside the Holy Place is the place of worship. The golden lampstand is one of the most perfect figures of Christ that we have. The table of showbread speaks of Him as being the Bread of Life. The altar of incense speaks of prayer—that the Lord is our great intercessor today, and we pray to the Father through Him.

The table of showbread has twelve loaves of bread on it. There are many explanations of how these loaves were arranged but the important thing to remember is that each loaf represents a tribe of Israel. In other words, God was providing equality for all.

Thou shalt also make a table of shittim wood: two cubits shall be the length thereof, and a cubit the breadth

thereof, and a cubit and a half the height thereof [Exod. 25:23].

You will notice that the table of showbread is two cubits long, and a cubit wide—twice as long as it is wide. It is a cubit and one half high. The table of showbread is the same height as the ark of the covenant.

And thou shalt overlay it with pure gold, and make thereto a crown of gold round about [Exod. 25:24].

The "crown of gold" is a border around the table to keep the bread from falling off.

And thou shalt make unto it a border of an hand breadth round about, and thou shalt make a golden crown to the border thereof round about.

And thou shalt make for it four rings of gold, and put the rings in the four corners that are on the four feet thereof [Exod. 25:25–26].

Once again we are told that staves were to be put through these rings in order that the table might be carried through the wilderness as the children of Israel journeyed. It was carried on the shoulders of the priests.

And thou shalt make the dishes thereof, and spoons thereof, and covers thereof, and bowls thereof, to cover withal: of pure gold shalt thou make them.

And thou shalt set upon the table shewbread before me alway [Exod. 25:29–30].

The bread is a type of Christ. Therefore the table is a type of Christ. It pictures Him. The table of showbread suggests many things: it speaks of sustenance, provision, and supply. It is the table of salvation. Our Lord gave a parable in Matthew 22:1–14 which tells about the marriage of the king's son. The invited guests refused to come, and this provoked the king to deal with the rejectors. Having done so, the king extended the invitation to include those in the highways and byways. They were bidden to come and eat. Thus the invitation has gone out today to the world to come and partake of the salvation as it is in the Lord Jesus Christ.

It is also a table of provision. God, as Creator, provides all food for man and beast. Whether you like it or not, friend, you eat every day at God's table in the physical realm. Yet how few recognize this truth and give thanks to Him for His bounty. God is the one who provides for us.

This table also speaks of the Lord's Supper, as instituted by the Lord Himself just prior to His death upon the Cross. It is a table for believers. The table of showbread is a prefiguration of Christ as the sustainer of spiritual life for the believer.

The table was two cubits long, one cubit wide, and one and one half cubits high. It was made of shittim wood and overlaid with gold. The almost incorruptible shittim (acacia) wood speaks of His human-ity. This wood was a product of the earth but was not subject to the action of it in a chemical way. In the same way our Lord had a body made of earth elements and conceived in the womb of a virgin. The gold speaks of His deity, but the gold is not produced by the earth; it is separate from it and has an inherent value. Christ was not of the earth in His deity. He was God. He came from glory.

On the table were placed twelve loaves of bread. The table and the bread are spoken of as one. We do the same thing today when we say, "The Lord's table." We do not eat the table, but we associate the table with the food. This metonymy is common in Scripture.

The bread was changed each Sabbath. The bread which was re-moved was eaten with wine by the priestly family in the Holy Place. This table doesn't prefigure Christ in the same way that manna does. Although both speak of Christ, it is not in the same connection. The manna speaks of Christ as the *life-giver*. He interpreted this Himself in John 6:32 when He said, ". . . Verily, verily, I say unto you, Moses gave you not that bread from heaven; but my Father giveth you the true bread from heaven." A short time later, in John 6:35, Jesus said, ". . . I am the bread of life: he that cometh to me shall never hunger; and he that believeth on me shall never thirst."

Now the showbread also speaks of Christ as the *life-sustainer*. Eternal life is a gift and is the manna which came down from heaven. The person who receives manna receives eternal life. However, eternal life requires a special food to sustain it and help it grow and find strength. The showbread pictures Christ as that special food for those who have partaken of the manna of life.

The Lord Jesus Christ is seen in another illustration that He also used. The showbread was made of grain which was ground and unleavened, made into bread and baked. Leviticus 24:5 says, "And thou shalt take fine flour, and bake twelve cakes thereof: two tenth deals shall be in one cake." Then we find that the Lord Jesus said, "Verily, verily, I say unto you, Except a corn of wheat fall into the ground and die, it abideth alone: but if it die, it bringeth forth much fruit" (John 12:24). The Lord Jesus Christ was ground in the mill of suffering. In His anguish Christ said in John 12:27, "Now is my soul troubled; and what shall I say? Father, save me from this hour: but for this cause came I unto this hour." John 12:31–32 tells us that He was brought into the fire of suffering and judgment. "Now is the judgment of this world: now shall the prince of this world be cast out. And I, if I be lifted up from the earth, will draw all men unto me." Jesus Christ came forth from the tomb in newness of life because His soul did not see corruption. Now He lives a resurrection life. He is the showbread now for believers to feed upon to sustain eternal life and promote growth. The Christian is to feed upon the living Christ. He is to appropriate Christ as He is today, living at God's right hand. Jesus Christ said, ". . . I am the bread of life . . ." (John 6:35).

There is an ancient proverb which contains the thought that a thing grows by what it feeds upon. And a book on the subject of dieting is entitled, *You Are What You Eat*. The difficulty today is that we have too many Christians who are not feeding upon Christ. You have to feed on Him in order to grow. In 2 Corinthians 5:16 Paul tells us, "Wherefore henceforth know we no man after the flesh: yea, though we have known Christ after the flesh, yet now henceforth know we him no more." We no longer know Christ after the flesh. We must feed upon Him as He is today. He is the living Christ and we are to grow by looking to Him.

THE GOLDEN LAMPSTAND

The next article of furniture is the lampstand, in most translations called the candlestick, but it was really a lampstand.

And thou shalt make a candlestick of pure gold: of beaten work shall the candlestick be made: his shaft, and his branches, his bowls, his knops, and his flowers, shall be of the same.

And six branches shall come out of the sides of it; three branches of the candlestick out of the one side, and three branches of the candlestick out of the other side:

Three bowls made like unto almonds, with a knop and a flower in one branch; and three bowls made like almonds in the other branch, with a knop and a flower: so in the six branches that come out of the candlestick [Exod. 25:31–33].

As the description continues from verses 34–39, the reading becomes rather tedious. Verse 40 says:

And look that thou make them after their pattern, which was shewed thee in the mount [Exod. 25:40].

The lampstand is probably the most perfect picture of Christ found in the tabernacle furniture. It sets Him forth as pure gold and speaks of His deity. It sets Him forth as He is—*God*. Worship has to do with walking in the light. This is a very important fact to see.

We have studied the table of showbread and have seen that it spoke of the fact that when we worship God we must feed on the Lord Jesus Christ. If you go to church and you are only entertained, or given a book review, or listen to some social issue being debated, or hear how you can improve your city, you are not having a worship service. You are just having a meeting. You only worship God when you feed upon Him who is the table of showbread.

Now in order to worship God, you must also walk in the light. Christ is the light, as symbolized by the lampstand in the Holy Place. If you wanted natural light, you had to go outside the tabernacle. If you wanted to walk in the light of the lampstand, you had to go inside the tabernacle. John 1:9 tells us that Jesus Christ is the ". . . true Light, which lighteth every man that cometh into the world." You will find that there are people who counsel others by "words." We are told that through philosophy and vain deceit we can be deceived. Listen to the words of Paul in Colossians 2:8, "Beware lest any man spoil you through philosophy and vain deceit, after the tradition of men, after the rudiments of the world, and not after Christ." Christ is not just another philosopher who "darkened counsel by words without knowledge." He is the Son of God, and in Him there is no darkness at all.

The lampstand was actually made of one piece of gold. It was beaten work, highly ornamented. It had a central shaft, but extending from that shaft were three branches on each side, making a total of seven branches in all. Each branch was like the limb of an almond tree with fruit and blossom. At the top was an open almond blossom, and it was here that the lamps filled with oil were placed.

The almond blossoms looked like wood but they were gold. They remind us of Aaron's rod that budded. When Aaron's priestly prerogative was in question, the budding of his almond rod established his right to the priesthood. The almond rod, a dead branch, was made to live and bear fruit. Christ was established as the Son of God by His resurrection from the dead. The resurrection did not make Christ the Son of God because He was already that from the eternal counsels of God; the resurrection only confirmed it. Aaron was the God-appointed high priest, and this position was confirmed by the resurrection of the dead almond rod. The resurrection of Christ likewise established His priesthood. Christ is our great High Priest. He became a man and partook of our nature, "tempted in all points as we are, yet without sin." But the primary basis of His priesthood is His deity. The priest represented man before God. And Christ, as God who became man, is now the God-man who represents man. There is Someone in heaven who knows and understands me! He is able to help me. The resurrection which declared Him to be the Son of God likewise declared His right to the priesthood.

It is interesting to note that no measurements are given for the lampstand. Why? Because you can't put a yardstick down on Deity, friend. You cannot measure Him as the Son of God. You can't understand Him. He is beyond the computation of man. Yet He also was perfectly human. His deity and humanity are never fused. Along with the fact that Jesus wept was the fact that He commanded Lazarus to come forth.

The lampstand gave light in the Holy Place. It was the place of worship. Notice that the lampstand held up the lighted lamps. In turn, the lamps revealed the beauty of the lampstand. The oil in the lamps represents the Holy Spirit. Christ said of the Holy Spirit in John 14:26, "But the Comforter, which is the Holy Ghost, whom the Father will send in my name, he shall teach you all things, and bring all things to your remembrance, whatsoever I have said unto you." When you and I study the Word together, we meet around the person of Christ, and it is the Holy Spirit who takes the things of Christ and shows them unto us—just as those lamps reveal the beauty of the lampstand. The Holy Spirit reveals Christ as the Son of God, the One who came to earth on our behalf and who lives in heaven to intercede for us.

CHAPTER 26

THEME: The curtains of the tabernacle; the boards and sockets of the tabernacle; the veils

THE CURTAINS OF THE TABERNACLE

Over the tabernacle proper were four coverings. The first covering was linen and it covered that part of the tabernacle that was 30 cubits long, 10 cubits wide, and 10 cubits high. This linen covering came down the sides of the tabernacle but was not permitted to touch the ground.

> Moreover thou shalt make the tabernacle with ten curtains of fine twined linen, and blue, and purple, and scarlet: with cherubims of cunning work shalt thou make them [Exod. 26:1].

The linen covering was beautiful and the result of fine work.

> And thou shalt make curtains of goats' hair to be a covering upon the tabernacle: eleven curtains shalt thou make [Exod. 26:7].

These curtains had to be sewn together.

> The length of one curtain shall be thirty cubits, and the breadth of one curtain four cubits: and the eleven curtains shall be all of one measure [Exod. 26:8].

The length of one curtain was to be 30 cubits which means it would exactly cover the top and sides of the tabernacle. They were held together with loops and rings.

> And thou shalt make a covering for the tent of rams' skins dyed red, and a covering above of badgers' skins [Exod. 26:14].

The third covering was made of rams' skins dyed red and the fourth covering was badgers' skins, or more correctly, sealskins. The women used to wear sealskin coats and this tabernacle was probably the first one that ever wore a sealskin coat!

Now each of these coverings had symbolic meaning. The first covering was fine-twined, Egyptian linen with cherubim woven in the material. It did not touch the ground, and its beauty could only be seen on the inside of the tabernacle. This covering could not be seen from the outside at all and, frankly, the beauty of the Lord Jesus Christ can not be seen by the world. He can only satisfy His own people. It is important for believers to worship Him because we not only need to feed on Him, but we need to behold Him in His beauty. In Psalm 17:8, David said, "Keep me as the apple of the eye, hide me under the shadow of thy wings." The wings of the cherubim were woven in the linen cloth over the tabernacle. But under His wings is a good place for us to be hidden, and we should worship Him who is worthy of our worship.

The second curtain was made of goats' hair and it touched the ground. This curtain speaks of Christ's worth for sinners. It is symbolic of the death of Christ, and this is the message that is to be given to the world. We read in Hebrews 9:26, "For then must he often have suffered since the foundation of the world: but now once in the end of the world hath he appeared to put away sin by the sacrifice of himself." The word world in this verse is better translated "age." He has appeared, and this is the message that should go forth. This is the story which the goats' hair curtain tells.

The third covering was made of rams' skin dyed red. This curtain speaks of the strength and vigor of Christ and His offering on the Cross. This curtain shows the outward aspect of His offering as our substitute.

The fourth curtain was made of badgers' skins (sealskins). After forty years in the wilderness this curtain was marred by time and weather, but it always protected that which was within. This covering speaks of Christ's walk before men. Just as the linen covering was inside to show His beauty to the believer, so the sealskin covering had no beauty to reveal. Isaiah 53:2 tells us this about Christ: ". . . he hath no form nor comeliness; and when we shall see him, there is no beauty that we should desire him." There is no beauty on the outside that we should desire Him; we have to go inside to behold His beauty. The world does not see in Him what we see in Him.

THE BOARDS AND SOCKETS OF THE TABERNACLE

And thou shalt make boards for the tabernacle of shittim wood standing up.

Ten cubits shall be the length of a board, and a cubit and a half shall be the breadth of one board.

Two tenons shall there be in one board, set in order one against another: thus shalt thou make for all the boards of the tabernacle.

And thou shalt make the boards for the tabernacle, twenty boards on the south side southward.

And thou shalt make forty sockets of silver under the twenty boards; two sockets under one board for his two tenons, and two sockets under another board for his two tenons [Exod. 26:15–19].

These boards were made of shittim wood which was a very durable wood like redwood. It was practically indestructible. These boards were covered with gold. There were twenty boards on each side and ten in the rear of the tabernacle. There was a certain amount of overlapping, of course, but this actually constituted the tabernacle proper. Rings were placed in the boards and bars ran through the rings, thus holding the tabernacle together.

Everything in the tabernacle speaks of either the person or work of Christ. Every covering, every thread, and every article of furniture reveals some facet of the Savior. As the bars held the tabernacle together, so the Holy Spirit of God holds true believers together today. Believers should be held together by the Spirit. In fact, believers are told "to keep the unity of the Spirit in the bond of peace."

The curtains covering the tabernacle each bore a different color and each had its own significance. There was blue, a heavenly color. There was scarlet, which speaks of Christ's blood. There was a blending of the blue and scarlet which produced a purple color that speaks of royalty. The blue and scarlet speak of heaven touching earth, or the humanity of Christ. The purple speaks of Him as King of the Jews. The boards, bars, and rings were overlaid with gold which speaks of the deity of the Lord Jesus Christ.

THE VEILS

And thou shalt make a veil of blue, and purple, and scarlet, and fine twined linen of cunning work: with cherubims shall it be made:

And thou shalt hang it upon four pillars of shittim wood overlaid with gold: their hooks shall be of gold, upon the four sockets of silver [Exod. 26:31–32].

The veil was hung upon four pillars and speaks of the humanity of Jesus Christ. The pillars were made of shittim wood covered with gold, with silver sockets attached. These speak of deity taking hold of earth through redemption. There was no capital on top of these pillars, which made them different from the other pillars in the tabernacle; they were just cut off. Isaiah 53:8 tells us, "He was taken from prison and from judgment: and who shall declare his generation? for he was cut off out of the land of the living: for the transgression of my people was he stricken." Jesus Christ was cut off out of the land of the living—He lived to be only thirty-three years old.

Now the veil was made of fine-twined linen and was the only entrance to the Holy of Holies. The veil speaks of the humanity of Christ. When Christ was on the Cross, He dismissed His spirit. At the moment of His death the veil was torn in two, representing the fracture of His spirit and His body. When the veil in the temple was rent in two, the way into God's presence was open. The only way to get to God today is through the Lord Jesus Christ. There is only one entrance to the Holy of Holies and only one way to God. In John 14:6 Jesus Himself said, ". . . I am the way, the truth, and the life: no man cometh unto the Father, but by me."

Some people believe that you can come to God if you are sincere and belong to some church. Do not believe it. You will not find this type of thinking in the Word of God.

What a wonderful picture the veil is. It shows the humanity of Christ. Friends, it is the death of Jesus Christ that saves us. His spotless life condemns us. When I stand before the veil, I am condemned. I see myself as not able to pass into the presence of God. We read in Matthew 27:50-51 that, "Jesus, when he had cried again with a loud voice, yielded up the ghost. And, behold, the veil of the temple was rent in twain from the top to the bottom; and the earth did quake, and the rocks rent." The death of Jesus Christ provides access to God, and the rent veil pictures it.

Then there is another hanging:

> And thou shalt make an hanging for the door of the tent, of blue, and purple, and scarlet, and fine twined linen, wrought with needlework.

> And thou shalt make for the hanging five pillars of shittum wood, and overlay them with gold, and their hooks shall be of gold: and thou shalt cast five sockets of brass for them [Exod. 26:36-37].

This veil, or hanging, led to the Holy Place, the place of worship where the golden lampstand, table of showbread, and altar of incense were located. Now, friend, we cannot worship God any old way. We have to come in spirit and in truth. Jesus said, ". . . I am the way, the truth, and the life: no man cometh unto the Father, but by me" (John 14:6).

Both veils prefigure our Lord Jesus Christ.

CHAPTER 27

THEME: The brazen altar; the court of the tabernacle; oil for the lamp

Notice now as we move outside the tabernacle proper to the court that the articles of furniture are made of brass: the brazen altar and the brazen laver. Inside, you recall, the articles of furniture were of gold. As you get closer to God, the emphasis is on the person of Christ. As you move farther out, the emphasis is on the work of Christ.

THE BRAZEN ALTAR

And thou shalt make an altar of shittim wood, five cubits long, and five cubits broad; the altar shall be foursquare: and the height thereof shall be three cubits.

And thou shalt make the horns of it upon the four corners thereof: his horns shall be of the same: and thou shalt overlay it with brass.

And thou shalt make his pans to receive his ashes, and his shovels, and his basins, and his fleshhooks, and his firepans: all the vessels thereof thou shalt make of brass [Exod. 27:1–3].

The furniture in the outer court is made of brass which represents judgment of sin. The sin question must be settled in the court before entrance can be made into the Holy Place. The furniture in the Holy Place was all of gold and pictures communion with God and worship of God. There is no sin in the Holy Place. The sin question is dealt with in the outer court.

Man is standing on the outside. How is he going to approach God? The first thing he must have is a substitute to die for him. Man might avoid meeting God, but if he wants to meet God and not die, he must have a substitute. Someone will have to die on that brazen altar for him. Sometimes this altar is called the table of the Lord, and it is called the altar of burnt offering. This is where God deals with the sinner. It speaks of the Cross of Christ, and of the fact that He is actually the One who died in man's stead. It is as Paul said in Ephesians 5:2, "And walk in love, as Christ also hath loved us, and hath given himself for us an offering and a sacrifice to God for a sweet-smelling savour." Christ is our burnt offering. The altar was made by man, but the pattern is in heaven. The Cross was God's chosen altar of sacrifice. The Lord Jesus Christ was delivered by the determinate counsel and foreknowledge of God to die on the Cross. Christ, therefore, is more than just a good man. He is that and also He is the Lamb slain from the foundation of the world. There is no approach to God except by the brazen altar. There a victim must be sacrificed and must be claimed as the substitute. John 1:29 tells us, "The next day John seeth Jesus coming unto him, and saith, Behold the Lamb of God, which taketh away the sin of the world." The apostle John spoke of Christ as that substitute upon the brazen altar. That is what the Cross became in those last three hours when darkness descended and Christ paid for the sins of the world.

We are told in John 1:12 that ". . . as many as received him, to them gave he power to become the sons of God, even to them that believe on his name." Man could not worship, pray, or serve God until he came to the brazen altar. Every priest, every Levite, had to come to this altar. Friends, "the way of the cross leads home." If Jesus Christ had not gone by the brazen altar, we would have no access to God.

Jesus Christ is not only the Lamb that died for us, He is also the risen Lamb. The apostle John tells us in Revelation 5:6 that he saw a ". . . Lamb as it had been slain . . ." The brazen altar stood at the entrance of the tabernacle. The Cross of Christ stands before heaven— it was raised on this earth but there is no entrance to heaven except by this Cross.

The brass which covered the altar speaks of judgment. The shittim wood covered with brass speaks of His strength for sacrifice. What a picture this is of the Cross of Christ!

THE COURT OF THE TABERNACLE

And thou shalt make the court of the tabernacle: for the south side southward there shall be hangings for the court of fine twined linen of an hundred cubits long for one side:

And for the gate of the court shall be an hanging of twenty cubits, of blue, and purple, and scarlet, and fine twined linen, wrought with needlework: and their pillars shall be four, and their sockets four [Exod. 27:9, 16].

Once again the colors of the hangings tell a story. Blue was a heavenly color and spoke of the fact that Christ came from heaven. Scarlet spoke of Christ's humanity and the blood that He shed for mankind. The purple was a blending of the blue and scarlet, the color of royalty, speaking of Christ's kingship. This was the hanging for the gate of the court through which the priests and Levites entered. This entrance was only five cubits high, and the fence that went around the outside of the tabernacle was one hundred cubits by fifty cubits, and was covered with white linen all the way around. It separated those on the inside from those on the outside.

OIL FOR THE LAMP

The conclusion of this chapter is quite interesting. It deals with the oil for the lamp, and it is unusual that this subject should be brought up at this particular place.

And thou shalt command the children of Israel, that they bring thee pure oil olive beaten for the light, to cause the lamp to burn always [Exod. 27:20].

Oil, as has already been pointed out, speaks of the Holy Spirit of God—Zechariah's interpretation of the lampstand: ". . . Not by might, nor by power, but by my *spirit* saith the Lord of hosts" (Zech. 4:6). The *light* is that which the Holy Spirit gives. The Holy Spirit will not speak of Himself, but He takes the things of Christ and shows them unto us.

In the tabernacle of the congregation without the veil, which is before the testimony, Aaron and his sons shall order it from evening to morning before the LORD: it shall be a statute for ever unto their generations on the behalf of the children of Israel [Exod. 27:21].

The burning light speaks of Christ. Now all that has changed—the Lord Jesus Christ has gone back to heaven. Matthew 5:14 tells us: "Ye are the light of the world. . . ." You and I do not make much light. It is only the Spirit of God that can use us. The first picture we have of Christ in the Book of Revelation shows Him walking in the midst of the lampstands. He is trying to keep the church's light of witness alive and burning on earth. Christ is dealing with those who are His own.

A word or two should be said about two articles of furniture not yet mentioned. One piece of furniture is the altar of incense which is mentioned over in Exodus chapter 30. If you were going to worship God, you had to come by this altar.

The other article of furniture not yet mentioned is the brazen laver. The laver made one clean to worship God. At the brazen altar you received Jesus Christ as Savior, and at the brazen laver you are washed and cleansed by the Holy Spirit of God. Then you are permitted to go and worship God.

CHAPTER 28

THEME: Aaron and his sons set apart for the priesthood; the ephod; the breastplate; the Urim and
Thummim; the robe of the ephod

AARON AND HIS SONS SET APART
FOR THE PRIESTHOOD

We have seen that every thread, color, and chord in the tabernacle
suggest the person and work of Christ. Now we come to the
ones who are going to serve in the tabernacle. The Levites were to care
for the tabernacle, and Aaron and his sons were to be the priests.
Aaron was to be the high priest.

**And take thou unto thee Aaron thy brother, and his sons
with him, from among the children of Israel, that he
may minister unto me in the priest's office, even Aaron,
Nadab and Abihu, Eleazar and Ithamar, Aaron's sons.**

**And thou shalt make holy garments for Aaron thy
brother for glory and for beauty [Exod. 28:1–2].**

In order for Aaron to serve as high priest he had to have certain garments. And these garments speak of Christ. It is true that most of the
instructions given in Exodus do not make very thrilling reading, nor
do they read like a detective or a mystery story, but they do reveal
Christ. Do you wonder why God gave us all of these instructions?
Little children learn by pictures. The Bible is a picture book and God
wants us to learn the truths He has for us by looking at the "pictures"
He has given us.

These garments were not holy in the sense that you and I think of
holy today. The Hebrew word for *holy* means "set apart." These garments were set apart for the service of God. Anything that is set apart
for God is holy.

Suppose you have ten dollars in your pocketbook and you want to give one dollar to the Lord's work. You may have received that ten dollars from a store, and the store may have received it from a gambler, who in turn may have received it from a prostitute, who may have gotten it from a thief and so on. But the minute you set that money aside for God, it is holy. Anything set aside for God is holy.

These are holy garments and are to be used in the service of God. I do not wear a robe like the Levites used to wear but when I was a pastor I had a mohair suit which I wore exclusively in the pulpit. I had a great deal of fun kidding my intimate friends about my "holy suit." When I preach, I have on my holy clothes and, in one sense, I am accurate because anything set aside for the service of God is holy.

Notice that these are for the glory of God and they are beautiful. I love that. Things do not have to be ugly, friends, just because they are used in the service of God. I personally resent that the world, the flesh, and the Devil seem to get everything that is beautiful. Why can't we give God some of the beauty? He is the one who made beauty. If you do not think He splashes color around, watch a sunset, or look at the leaves in the fall. Look at the heavens during a clear sunny day and then watch them during a storm. God majors in colors and beauty, and these garments for the priests were to be beautiful and for the glory of God.

And thou shalt speak unto all that are wise-hearted, whom I have filled with the spirit of wisdom, that they may make Aaron's garments to consecrate him, that he may minister unto me in the priest's office [Exod. 28:3].

Aaron is to be set aside for the ministry of the great high priest. These are to be his garments:

And these are the garments which they shall make; a breastplate, and an ephod, and a robe, and a broidered coat, a mitre, and a girdle: and they shall make holy garments for Aaron thy brother, and his sons, that he may minister unto me in the priest's office [Exod. 28:4].

Here are six garments that are to be used in the service of God. They are to be worn by Aaron and then, of course, passed on to those who shall succeed him in the office.

And they shall take gold, and blue, and purple, and scarlet, and fine linen [Exod. 28:5].

These garments are to be made out of the very best material. I feel like God ought to have the very best, but I must confess that we need to be very careful about this subject. Never in my ministry have I driven an automobile that is considered expensive, like a Cadillac or a Lincoln. One time a man offered to buy me an expensive car and I refused. I happen to drive a Chevrolet but, quite frankly, I feel I have as much right to drive a Cadillac. Now this is where I must be careful. Right now I know a certain minister who is coming under great criticism because several people went out to his headquarters one day and found nothing but Cadillacs parked around the place. The type of ministry in which he is engaged begs and urges people to give money to his work and there are those who feel the money received is not being spent wisely.

May I say that money sent into a ministry should not be spent needlessly. We ought to be very careful what we do with contributions. I have attempted to follow a pattern of being very careful with money because I ask people to give to my radio ministry. For this reason I drive a Chevrolet. So if anyone is thinking about giving me a Cadillac, forget it. Seriously, we need to be careful. On the other hand, we should recognize that God's work should have the very best, and that does not necessarily mean a Cadillac.

When we moved into our new headquarters, we needed to settle the question of what kind of equipment we should have. Should the machine used to make the radio tapes be a cheap model? No! The tapes are very important and so we got the best machine we could find. We feel that good equipment for God's work is essential; God's work ought to have it. I trust that you understand what I am saying because I believe that God is being cheated and robbed. Malachi asked this question, "Will a man rob God? Yet ye have robbed me. But ye say,

Wherein have we robbed thee? In tithes and offerings" (Mal. 3:8). God knows that a man will rob Him. Man was that way in Moses' day and man is still the same today.

THE EPHOD

And they shall make the ephod of gold, of blue, and of purple, of scarlet, and fine twined linen, with cunning work.

It shall have the two shoulderpieces thereof joined at the two edges thereof; and so it shall be joined together.

And the curious girdle of the ephod, which is upon it, shall be of the same, according to the work thereof; even of gold, of blue, and purple, and scarlet, and fine twined linen.

And thou shalt take two onyx stones, and grave on them the names of the children of Israel [Exod. 28:6-9].

The ephod is difficult to describe. It was worn over the linen garment. Two long pieces of cloth were brought together and fastened by a stone on one shoulder and a stone on the other shoulder. The material was gathered in the middle with a girdle. Six of the names of the children of Israel were engraved on one onyx stone and six names were engraved on the other. When the high priest went into the presence of God, he carried the children of Israel on his shoulders. That speaks of the strength and power of the high priest. Hebrews 7:25 tells us about Jesus Christ our High Priest: "Wherefore he is able also to save them to the uttermost that come unto God by him, seeing he ever liveth to make intercession for them." Christ is able to save us, you see. He has strength and power.

Do you remember the parable He gave about the little lost sheep? The shepherd went out and found him and put him on his shoulders (Luke 15:1-7). Jesus Christ carries me on His shoulders and that is where He carries you, friend. From time to time I get off His shoulders but He is right there to lift me back to that place of safety and continue to carry me. What a lovely picture the ephod gives us of Christ.

THE BREASTPLATE

And thou shalt make the breastplate of judgment with cunning work; after the work of the ephod thou shalt make it; of gold, of blue, and of purple, and of scarlet, and of fine twined linen, shalt thou make it.

Foursquare it shall be being doubled; a span shall be the length thereof, and a span shall be the breadth thereof [Exod. 28:15–16].

The best way to describe the breastplate is to call it a vest—but a very beautiful one—that went over the garment. It was a breastplate of judgment. Why? Well, friends, it pictures the fact that sin has been judged. We need the breastplate of righteousness today as believers. You see, the breastplate covers the vile heart within us. That is the only way we could stand in the presence of God. It means that our sins are judged. The righteousness of Christ has been made over to us. So this is called the breastplate of judgment.

The breastplate was, in a way, part of the ephod. The ephod and the breastplate went together and was a thing of beauty.

And thou shalt set in it settings of stones, even four rows of stones: the first row shall be a sardius, a topaz, and a carbuncle: this shall be the first row.

And the second row shall be an emerald, a sapphire, and a diamond.

And the third row a ligure, an agate, and an amethyst.

And the fourth row a beryl, and an onyx, and a jasper: they shall be set in gold in their inclosings [Exod. 28:17–20].

On the breastplate of the great high priest were these twelve precious stones which were arranged three in a row, and there were four rows.

And the stones shall be with the names of the children of Israel, twelve, according to their names, like the engravings of a signet; every one with his name shall they be according to the twelve tribes [Exod. 28:21].

These stones are also found in the Book of Revelation where we are told that they form the foundation of the New Jerusalem. Each stone was a different color and together they formed a flashing and beautiful display. I am of the opinion that God's universe is filled with color, and when sin is finally removed we will see it flash with color.

These twelve stones are quite interesting. When the high priest went into God's presence wearing the breastplate, he pictured the Lord Jesus Christ who is at the right hand of God interceding for us. The Lord not only carries us on His shoulders, the place of power and ability, but He carries us on His breast. We are engraven on His heart. He loves us! What a picture this is of His love for us.

THE URIM AND THUMMIM

And thou shalt put in the breastplate of judgment the Urim and the Thummim; and they shall be upon Aaron's heart, when he goeth in before the LORD: and Aaron shall bear the judgment of the children of Israel upon his heart before the LORD continually [Exod. 28:30].

I am going to tell you a secret and I do not want you to tell anyone. I do not know what the Urim and the Thummim were. I have read books by about twenty-five different authors and have discovered that they do not know either. The interesting thing is that they had something to do with determining the will of God. Just how, I do not know. Some people think the Urim and Thummim were dice, but I do not believe it. Whatever they were, they determined the will of God. God has kept the details obscure for a very good reason—some nut would try to produce a Urim and Thummim today and would claim that it would give us all the answers. We have a lot of people around today trying to give us the answers without the Urim and Thummim! God wants us to go to Him for the answers.

THE ROBE OF THE EPHOD

And beneath upon the hem of it thou shalt make pomegranates of blue, and of purple, and of scarlet, round about the hem thereof; and bells of gold between them round about:

A golden bell and a pomegranate, a golden bell and a pomegranate, upon the hem of the robe round about [Exod. 28:33–34].

The first sermon I preached in California was on the golden bells and pomegranates. I told the congregation I did not know exactly what a pomegranate was. Well, I found that they are grown in Southern California. By nine o'clock that evening I had at least twenty bushels of pomegranates on my back porch! I know what they are now.

The pomegranates speak of fruit, and the bells speak of witness. We should have both of these in our lives. We ought to be a witness for Christ, and there ought to be the fruit of the Holy Spirit (Gal. 5:22–23) in our lives. You should not be handing out tracts, friends, unless you are making the right kind of "tracks" in this world. Too many people want to witness but do not have a life to back it up. There are also some folk who have a life to back up a witness, but who do not witness. We ought to have a bell and a pomegranate, a bell and a pomegranate.

And it shall be upon Aaron to minister: and his sound shall be heard when he goeth in unto the holy place before the LORD, and when he cometh out, that he die not [Exod. 28:35].

These symbols of life and witness would give a sound as the high priest went in and out of the sanctuary. "That he die not" alerts them to the fact that if he should default in the ritual he would be stricken dead.

> And thou shalt make a plate of pure gold, and grave upon it, like the engravings of a signet, HOLINESS TO THE LORD.
>
> And thou shalt put it on a blue lace, that it may be upon the mitre; upon the forefront of the mitre it shall be.
>
> And it shall be upon Aaron's forehead, that Aaron may bear the iniquity of the holy things, which the children of Israel shall hallow in all their holy gifts; and it shall be always upon his forehead, that they may be accepted before the LORD [Exod. 28:36–38].

These garments distinguished the high priest from the other priests, and they set forth the glories and beauties of our High Priest who is "holy, harmless, undefiled, separate from sinners." He died down here to save us. He lives at God's right hand to keep us saved.

> And thou shalt embroider the coat of fine linen, and thou shalt make the mitre of fine linen, and thou shalt make the girdle of needlework.
>
> And for Aaron's sons thou shalt make coats, and thou shalt make for them girdles, and bonnets shalt thou make for them, for glory and for beauty.
>
> And thou shalt put them upon Aaron thy brother, and his sons with him; and shalt anoint them, and conse- crate them, and sanctify them, that they may minister unto me in the priest's office.
>
> And thou shalt make them linen breeches to cover their nakedness; from the loins even unto the thighs they shall reach:

And they shall be upon Aaron, and upon his sons, when
they come in unto the tabernacle of the congregation, or
when they come near unto the altar to minister in the
holy place; that they bear not iniquity, and die: it shall
be a statute for ever unto him and his seed after him
[Exod. 28:39–43].

God wanted no nudity in the service for Him (and we should keep this
in mind for today). God wanted no display of the flesh. These garments were a covering over any work of the flesh.

CHAPTER 29

THEME: The consecration of the priests; the sacrifices of the consecration; the food of the priests; the continual burnt offering

THE CONSECRATION OF THE PRIESTS

Chapter 29 is a long chapter, and not all of it is as interesting and thrilling reading as it might be. I am confident, however, that the Spirit of God wants to use it to minister to us. This is God's *A-B-C Book* for us and it contains great spiritual lessons.

> And this is the thing that thou shalt do unto them to hallow them, to minister unto me in the priest's office: Take one young bullock, and two rams without blemish [Exod. 29:1].

Consecration for a believer is nothing that *he* does for himself. It is something that God does for him. It rests upon the finished work of Christ. It *has* to rest there.

> And unleavened bread, and cakes unleavened tempered with oil, and wafers unleavened anointed with oil: of wheaten flour shalt thou make them.
>
> And thou shalt put them into one basket, and bring them in the basket, with the bullock and the two rams.
>
> And Aaron and his sons thou shalt bring unto the door of the tabernacle of the congregation, and shalt wash them with water [Exod. 29:2–4].

The washing is typical of regeneration. Titus 3:5 tells us it is: "Not by works of righteousness which we have done, but according to his mercy he saved us, by the washing of regeneration, and renewing of the Holy Ghost." The washing mentioned in this passage has to do with regeneration. The laver deals with a different type of washing altogether.

Now Moses is going to put the garments upon Aaron.

And thou shalt take the garments, and put upon Aaron the coat, and the robe of the ephod, and the ephod, and the breastplate, and gird him with the curious girdle of the ephod:

And thou shalt put the mitre upon his head, and put the holy crown upon the mitre.

Then shalt thou take the anointing oil, and pour it upon his head, and anoint him.

And thou shalt bring his sons, and put coats upon them.

And thou shalt gird them with girdles, Aaron and his sons, and put the bonnets on them: and the priest's office shall be theirs for a perpetual statute: and thou shalt consecrate Aaron and his sons [Exod. 29:5–9].

Consecration is what God does rather than what we do. I hear so much today about "consecration services" where people promise to do something. I have promised God big things in the past and have never quite made good. I do not like to think of that as being consecration. It is not what I promise Him. Rather, consecration is coming to God with empty hands, confessing our weakness and our inability to do anything, then letting God do the rest.

If you read the prayers of Moses, Elijah, David, and Samuel in the Old Testament, and Paul in the New Testament, you will find that these men never came to God on the basis of what they were, who they were, or what they promised God that they would do. I have attended dedication services for years. I have watched people put a little chip or limb on the fire and then give a testimony about the things they were going to do for God. I have heard enough promises at those services to turn the world upside down for God. Unfortunately, many of those promises are never kept because we really do not have much to offer God, do we? Maybe you have something to offer Him, but I do not. The thing is that we need to come to Him with empty hands and allow Him to fill them.

THE SACRIFICES OF THE CONSECRATION

And thou shalt cause a bullock to be brought before the tabernacle of the congregation: and Aaron and his sons shall put their hands upon the head of the bullock [Exod. 29:10].

The high priest and his family put their hands upon the bullock. There are many people who believe that the laying on of hands transmits something magical or spiritual. It does not. That is not the purpose of the laying on of hands. The only thing you can transfer to another man by the laying on of hands is disease germs. This is all that is passed on. The laying on of hands on an animal speaks of identification. When a sinner came up to the altar and put his hands on the head of the animal he had brought, it meant that the animal was taking his place.

In the church I served for many years we had over one hundred missionaries. When a missionary went to his or her field of service, we held a consecration service to set that missionary aside for service. We put our hands on them. So far I have never transferred anything to a missionary yet. The purpose for the service was identification. The missionaries were identified with us and they represented us on the field. I consider that when I put hands on a missionary, he is identified with me in the ministry, and I have a certain responsibility to pray for him and support him. The laying on of hands means identification.

The bullock took Aaron's place. It will die for him because he is a sinner. This is the burnt offering. In Leviticus we shall go over these offerings in detail. Even in the Garden of Eden there was a burnt offering. The altar that we have identified as the brazen altar is sometimes

called the altar of burnt offering because it was here that the main
sacrifice was offered. The main sacrifice, which was the burnt offering and the first one, sets forth the person of Christ—who He is. The
altar speaks of what He has done for us.

THE FOOD OF THE PRIESTS

And thou shalt take the breast of the ram of Aaron's consecration, and wave it for a wave offering before the
LORD: and it shall be thy part.

And thou shalt sanctify the breast of the wave offering,
and the shoulder of the heave offering, which is waved,
and which is heaved up, of the ram of the consecration,
even of that which is for Aaron, and of that which is for
his sons [Exod. 29:26–27].

Once again in Leviticus you will find that a part of an offering went
to Aaron and the priest as their part. You see, the Levites were appor-
tioned no land for farming in the nation, and this is the way God provided for their support. The Levites were to serve in the tabernacle
and later in the temple, and they would receive a part of the offering.

THE CONTINUAL BURNT OFFERING

The continual burnt offering was to be continually offered.

Now this is that which thou shalt offer upon the altar;
two lambs of the first year day by day continually.

The one lamb thou shalt offer in the morning; and the
other lamb thou shalt offer at even:

And with the one lamb a tenth deal of flour mingled
with the fourth part of an hin of beaten oil; and the
fourth part of an hin of wine for a drink offering [Exod.
29:38–40].

Once again the Book of Leviticus gives us the details of the continual burnt offering. This offering was a daily sacrifice; a lamb was offered in the morning and a lamb was offered in the evening. It speaks of the fact that the people needed a continual reminder that someone was needed to take their place and that their sin merited death. There must be the shedding of blood for sin.

The Book of Hebrews brings out this truth: "For then must he often have suffered since the foundation of the world: but now once in the end of the world hath he appeared to put away sin by the sacrifice of himself" (Heb. 9:26). This verse, of course, is speaking about the sacrifice of the Lord Jesus Christ. The blood of bulls, goats, and lambs could not take away sin, but the blood of Jesus Christ could. His sacrifice is adequate. The Lord has dealt adequately with sin. He died only once. Once in the end of the age He appeared to put away sin by the sacrifice of Himself.

CHAPTER 30

THEME: The altar of incense; the ransomed may worship; the cleansed may worship; the anointed may worship; the incense

THE ALTAR OF INCENSE

This is the great worship chapter. In looking at the first compartment of the tabernacle proper, the Holy Place, we see three articles of furniture. All speak of worship. We have already considered the lampstand and the table of showbread, but there is also an altar here. It is the altar of incense. The table of showbread and the golden lampstand typify God's people meeting and fellowshiping together. (This is *not* where you meet together and gossip, but where you feed on the person of Jesus Christ. It is a banquet.) The altar of incense is the place of prayer.

> And thou shalt make an altar to burn incense upon: of shittim wood shalt thou make it.
>
> A cubit shall be the length thereof, and a cubit the breadth thereof; foursquare shall it be: and two cubits shall be the height thereof: the horns thereof shall be of the same [Exod. 30:1–2].

The instructions tell us that this was a small altar.

> And thou shalt overlay it with pure gold, the top thereof, and the sides thereof round about, and the horns thereof; and thou shalt make unto it a crown of gold round about.
>
> And two golden rings shalt thou make to it under the crown of it, by the two corners thereof, upon the two sides of it shalt thou make it; and they shall be for places for the staves to bear it withal [Exod. 30:3–4].

Even this small piece of furniture had rings so that staves could be put through them and it could be carried upon the shoulders of the priest. In the Book of Numbers we are told that on the wilderness march the Levites carried the articles of furniture.

> **And thou shalt put it before the veil that is by the ark of the testimony, before the mercy seat that is over the testimony, where I will meet with thee [Exod. 30:6].**

This altar was placed right by the veil, and the ark and mercy seat were on the other side of the veil. It stood in the Holy Place, the place of worship.

> **And Aaron shall burn thereon sweet incense every morning: when he dresseth the lamps, he shall burn incense upon it.**

> **And when Aaron lighteth the lamps at even, he shall burn incense upon it, a perpetual incense before the LORD throughout your generations [Exod. 30:7–8].**

This was not an altar of sacrifice.

> **Ye shall offer no strange incense thereon, nor burnt sacrifice, nor meat offering; neither shall ye pour drink offering thereon [Exod. 30:9].**

Only incense, and only a certain kind of incense, was to be placed upon this altar. The priests would go in and burn incense every time they would light the lamps of the lampstand. This altar speaks of prayer, and we know this because the Bible uses incense as a symbol of prayer and praise in many places. David, for example, in Psalm 141:2 says, "Let my prayer be set forth before thee as incense. . . ." The Book of Revelation gives us this picture of incense: "And another angel came and stood at the altar, having a golden censer; and there was given unto him much incense, that he should offer it with the prayers of all saints upon the golden altar which was before the throne" (Rev. 8:3). Luke 1:9 tells us that "According to the custom of the priest's office, his [Zacharias'] lot was to burn incense when he went into the temple of the Lord." Zacharias was a member of the tribe of Levi and he served in the temple. He was serving at the altar of incense, according to this verse, and it was at the time of prayer. Dr. Luke opens the New Testament—chronologically—with Zacharias at the altar of incense. In other words, God broke His silence of four hundred years at the altar of incense by giving a message to Zacharias there.

Incense, therefore, is a figure of the Lord Jesus Christ, our Intercessor. Aaron ministered in the place of worship and Aaron is a figure of Christ in this particular sense, although Christ is actually a priest after the order of Melchizedek (Heb. 7). In Hebrews 9 we find a strange thing—the altar of incense is placed in the Holy of Holies. It looks as if the writer of Hebrews didn't know where it belonged! Why did he locate it in the Holy of Holies rather than in the Holy Place as it is in Exodus? Because when he wrote, the veil had been rent in two. Christ had offered Himself down here. His flesh had been rent, and He had died upon the Cross. But He ascended back to heaven, and the altar of incense is in heaven today. We come to God through Jesus Christ. He is our great Intercessor. Christ is in heaven, and the altar speaks of the place where He stands. When we come to God in prayer, we have to come through the Lord Jesus Christ.

I have heard lots of people say, "Now that I am saved, I can go directly to God." No, you cannot! You go to God through Christ. He is the One who brings us into the presence of God. Christ is in heaven praying for us. It was wonderful for the children of Israel to know that their high priest was in the tabernacle, at the altar of incense, praying for them. It is wonderful for us to know that Jesus Christ, our great High Priest, is praying for us.

Christ does not pray for the world. Did you know that? In His high priestly prayer He says, "I pray for them: I pray not for the world, but for them which thou hast given me; for they are thine" (John 17:9). You say, "Why doesn't He pray for the world?" Jesus Christ *died* for the world. And the Holy Spirit is down here to make the offer of Christ real to those who will receive Him. Christ could do no more than die for the sins of the world. He is in heaven praying for those who have received Him as Savior. I am glad that He is doing this because if He were not, we could not accomplish very much on earth. What a precious thing it is to have a great High Priest who prays for us. God hears our prayers because of who Christ is and what He did for us on the Cross.

Ephesians 1:6 says, "To the praise of the glory of his grace, wherein he hath made us accepted in the beloved." Because of Jesus Christ, God the Father accepts us in the Beloved. In Matthew 17:5, Mark 9:7, and Luke 9:35 God the Father said, "This is my beloved Son: hear him." We are not only to hear Him, we are to pray through Him. Jesus Christ told us in John 14:14: "If ye shall ask any thing in my name, I will do it." This is what it means to pray in the Spirit.

You will notice that this altar is separated from the other articles of furniture. Only the priest could worship here. Even King Uzziah was smitten with leprosy when he tried to intrude here (2 Chron. 26:16–21). Only priests can pray today—and every true believer in Christ is a priest. There is a great deal of sentimental rubbish told around today that a person can lead any sort of sinful life he pleases, reject Christ, and then in time of trouble, perhaps when his mother is in the hospital, this reprobate can get on his knees before God and expect an answer. Motion pictures have shown scenes like this, and some sentimental preachers talk about such things happening, but God says He will not answer prayers like this. Let us be very careful about this, friends. The altar of incense is where priests go. The only prayer a sinner can pray is "God be merciful to me, a sinner." God will hear and answer that prayer when it is offered to Him.

Exodus 30:8 tells us that there is to be "a perpetual incense before the LORD throughout your generations." There is to be continual praise to God. In 1 Thessalonians we are told to "pray without ceasing." The incense was to be upon the altar in the morning and the evening.

When the high priest went inside and offered incense on the altar, he spent some time in the tabernacle. That incense stayed upon his garments and when he came outside, the people could smell him. You might say that he was wearing the right kind of fragrance. When the great high priest walked by, people caught the fragrance. They said, "My, doesn't he smell good!" The trouble with most saints today is that they are not wearing the right kind of cologne. The right cologne is *prayer.* Let your prayers ascend before God as sweet incense, and it will permeate your garments—if you spend time in prayer.

THE RANSOMED MAY WORSHIP

When thou takest the sum of the children of Israel after their number, then shall they give every man a ransom for his soul unto the LORD, when thou numberest them; that there be no plague among them, when thou numberest them.

This they shall give, every one that passeth among them that are numbered, half a shekel after the shekel of the sanctuary: (a shekel is twenty gerahs:) an half shekel shall be the offering of the LORD [Exod. 30:12-13].

This is the second requirement of worship. There will be no plague among them because they are going to be redeemed. They were to be ransomed with silver. Silver is the metal of redemption and a type of redemption. Everyone that worshiped had to be redeemed. We hear a great deal today about public worship. Actually there is no such thing. Only the redeemed can worship, but the way is open to "whosoever will" for redemption.

THE CLEANSED MAY WORSHIP

Not only must worshipers be redeemed, they must also be cleansed. That brings us to the laver. The laver is located in the outer court and is made of brass, along with the brazen altar. This is where God settles the sin questions and where He deals with our sin. The brazen laver is where God deals with our sins as saints. Saints sometimes sin. This idea that saints are heavenly is just not true. As one anonymous poet has said:

> To dwell above
> With saints in love
> O that will be glory!
> But to stay below
> With saints I know
> That is another story!

And the LORD spake unto Moses saying,

Thou shalt also make a laver of brass, and his foot also of brass, to wash withal: and thou shalt put it between the tabernacle of the congregation and the altar, and thou shalt put water therein.

For Aaron and his sons shall wash their hands and their feet thereat:

When they go into the tabernacle of the congregation, they shall wash with water, that they die not; or when they come near to the altar to minister, to burn offering made by fire unto the LORD [Exod. 30:17–20].

The priest could not come into the tabernacle to serve unless he had first washed. The priest got contaminated when he was on the outside. When you go to church and do not enjoy the service, maybe it is not just because the preacher is dull. Maybe you are a dirty saint. When you have the combination of a dull preacher and a dirty saint, you do not have a very exciting service.

We get dirty in this world, and we cannot worship until we are cleansed. That is why the Lord washed the disciples' feet. He is still doing that today. We need to go to the laver, friends. That is the first thing the priest did. If they were going to the brazen altar, they washed

before and after. If they were going into the Holy Place, they washed
before they came in and washed when they came out. I am of the opinion that the matter of washing was very important. It was so important, in fact, that I can imagine one priest saying to another priest at
the laver, "How many times have you been here today?" The other
priest might reply, "Nearly a dozen times." And the first priest would
say, "Well, I've been up here over a dozen times. And look at my
hands—I have dishpan hands because I have washed so much. I wonder why God wants us to do this so often?" And Aaron, standing in
the background, might have said, "The Lord wants you to wash and
wash and wash so that you will *know* that you have to be holy. You
cannot worship Him, serve Him, or be of use to Him unless you have
been cleaned up."

The idea that a dirty saint can serve God acceptably simply is not
true. Every now and then you hear of some man getting involved with
a woman, and folk say, "My, I do not understand how a thing like that
can happen to one who is doing a great work for God." The man might
have been a preacher or a fine Christian worker, but if you check his
work, you will find out that it is wood, hay, and stubble. In
1 Corinthians 3:12–15 we learn that ". . . if any man build upon this
foundation gold, silver, precious stones, wood, hay, stubble; Every
man's work shall be made manifest: for the day shall declare it, because it shall be revealed by fire; and the fire shall try every man's
work of what sort it is. If any man's work abide which he hath built
thereupon, he shall receive a reward. If any man's work shall be
burned, he shall suffer loss: but he himself shall be saved; yet so as by
fire." His "great work" amounts to nothing in God's sight. God wants
us to be clean.

The priests were to wash in the brazen laver. We are to come to Him
in confession. First John 1:9 tells us that "If we confess our sins, he is
faithful and just to forgive us our sins, and to cleanse us from all un-
righteousness." This laver of brass pictures our sanctification. We
must wash if we are going to serve God. We must wash if we are going
to be used by God. We must be clean. Not only should our garments
smell like sweet incense, but our bodies should be washed with pure
water. The pure water is the Word of God.

The laver was made out of brass. The women brought their highly polished brass mirrors to make the laver. They did not have glass mirrors then. The mirrors revealed dirt and that was the purpose of the laver. The laver cleansed the priest, and the laver pictures the Word of God. The Bible is a mirror and when we look into it, our sin is revealed. We then need to confess that sin and be cleansed.

Now you are not to confess your sin publicly; you go to Jesus Christ in private. That laver is in heaven. I think that every Sunday, before we ever go inside the church, we should confess our sins for the week. Do not tell me that you don't get dirty. Your eyes get dirty. Your mind gets dirty. Your hands get dirty. Your feet get dirty. You get dirty all right. One of the big troubles in our churches today is that there is too much spiritual B.O. We need to confess our sins to Him and wash before we go in to worship. God does not accept worship until it comes from a cleansed heart nor will He accept service except from a cleansed heart.

THE ANOINTED MAY WORSHIP

And thou shalt make it an oil of holy ointment, an ointment compound after the art of the apothecary: it shall be an holy anointing oil.

And thou shalt anoint the tabernacle of the congregation therewith, and the ark of the testimony,

And the table and all his vessels . . . [Exod. 30:25–27a].

What is the anointing for us today? It is the anointing of the Holy Spirit. We have an anointing that enables us to understand the Word of God. That is the reason the Bible is being made real to so many today. It is not the teacher nor the preacher; it is the Spirit of God using the Word of God. Only the Spirit can anoint you. You do not have to go to some man and have him pour oil on you. You can go to God right now and say, "God, open my heart and mind and life to understand Your Word." First John 2:20 says, "But ye have an unction from the Holy

One, and ye know all things." The word "unction" means *anointing* and it is ours.

First John 2:27 goes on to say, "But the anointing which ye have received of him abideth in you, and ye need not that any man teach you: but as the same anointing teacheth you of all things, and is truth, and is no lie, and even as it hath taught you, ye shall abide in him." The Holy Spirit is the one who can open your mind and heart when you go to work with God to understand His Word. What a blessing He will bring to your heart! There are so many people today who are asking the questions, "What is life all about? What shall I do today? How shall I communicate my needs?" Oh my dear friends, ask God to let the Holy Spirit of God make real His Word to your hearts, and true joy will be yours.

THE INCENSE

And the LORD said unto Moses, Take unto thee sweet spices, stacte, and onycha, and galbanum; these sweet spices with pure frankincense: of each shall there be a like weight:

And thou shalt make it a perfume, a confection after the art of the apothecary, tempered together, pure and holy:

And thou shalt beat some of it very small, and put of it before the testimony in the tabernacle of the congregation . . . [Exod. 30:34–36a].

Now the incense, as we are told in verse 34, was made of sweet spices, stacte, and onycha, and galbanum, along with pure frankincense. Stacte was a resinous gum that oozed from trees on Mount Gilead. It was called the balm of Gilead. The onycha came from a species of shell fish that resembled a crab. The galbanum was taken from the leaves of a Syrian plant. These were blended with pure frankincense. It was a secret formula, long since lost. The mixture of these spices gave off a sweet incense, and it was not to be duplicated nor replaced.

And as for the perfume which thou shalt make, ye shall not make to yourselves according to the composition thereof: it shall be unto thee holy for the LORD.

Whosoever shall make like unto that, to smell thereto, shall even be cut off from his people [Exod. 30:37–38].

No one was to use this formula for himself. Neither would God accept any counterfeit.

The altar speaks to us of prayer and worship. It is a place where we are to offer our praise, thanksgiving, and our requests. It is not to be duplicated. This formula was not to be used in an attempt to try and make the incense or worship pleasing to the natural man. You cannot make worship pleasing to the natural man. We are to worship God in spirit and in truth. All sorts of things are used to try and trap people into going to church. Nothing but the Word of God should be used to accomplish this. Make sure that the Word of God is foremost, and that everything centers around the Word of God.

In closing, I want to mention again that there were two altars. The burnt altar is where God deals with a sinner. It speaks of the earth and the sin of man. The altar of incense speaks of heaven and holiness. The burnt altar speaks of what Christ did for us on earth. The incense altar speaks of what Christ is doing for us in heaven today. It also speaks of our prayers and our part in worship. It speaks of Christ who prays for us. He is the one who truly praises God and prays for us. He is the one who genuinely worships God for us. He is our intercessor.

How are we to learn to worship? Well, not at the bloody altar where you go as a sinner and take Christ as your Savior. You enter the Holy Place and come to the golden altar. There is no sacrifice there because the question was settled outside. When you worship God, the sin question has to be settled. The very basis rests upon the fact that this altar once a year was consecrated with blood. As believers, we are accepted in the Beloved before God. God hears our prayers because of what Christ has done.

CHAPTER 31

THEME:The call of Spirit-filled craftsmen; the Sabbath Day becomes a sign

THE CALL OF SPIRIT-FILLED CRAFTSMEN

This chapter seems to be a departure from the study of the tabernacle, but actually it is not. What we have here is an interval between the giving of the Law and the instructions of the tabernacle. Moses spent a great deal of time on Mt. Sinai, receiving all the instructions. The children of Israel became somewhat impatient while they were waiting for him to return. This chapter tells us about the workmen who made the tabernacle and about one in particular who was given a special gift for making the articles of furniture, especially the more difficult pieces.

And the LORD spake unto Moses, saying,

See, I have called by name Bezaleel the son of Uri, the son of Hur, of the tribe of Judah:

And I have filled him with the spirit of God, in wisdom, and in understanding, and in knowledge, and in all manner of workmanship,

To devise cunning works, to work in gold, and in silver, and in brass,

And in cutting of stones, to set them, and in carving of timber, to work in all manner of workmanship.

And I, behold, I have given with him Aholiab, the son of Ahisamach, of the tribe of Dan: and in the hearts of all that are wise-hearted I have put wisdom, that they may make all that I have commanded thee [Exod. 31:1–6].

These men and their helpers were given special gifts for craftsmanship. They made the tabernacle furniture and also the garments. The Spirit of God equipped them for their work. The question might arise as to the trade of Bezaleel before God called him to do this work. I believe craftsmanship was his trade, and that he worked with gold and silver and other delicate things. But he was given a special gift from God to do His work.

My feeling is that whatever a man is equipped to do, that is the thing he should do unless God makes it clear that he should do otherwise. I find today that there are those who cannot speak well before an audience and yet want to. I know several laymen who are determined that they are going to be speakers, but they are not equipped for it. They have no trace of the gift of speaking, but they stubbornly continue to speak when other useful gifts they have go to waste. I know a man in radio work who is a technical expert, but all he wants to do is speak. He has a special gift, and I think he should confine himself to the gift God has given him.

When I was a pastor in Nashville, one of the deacons of my church came to me the first day I arrived and asked me never to call on him for public prayer. "It scares me to death; I have stage fright and I cannot seem to overcome my fear. It must be abnormal, but I make a fool of myself when I try to speak in public," he said. This man was the superintendent of a street car company and held an executive position, but he confessed to me that he could not do any public speaking that made sense. He did tell me, however, that if there was anything that needed to be done around the church, to let him know. He turned out to be a wonderful helper and he was right there whenever I called on him. Before I left that church, I was thanking God that this man did not have the gift of public speaking because it made him faithful to the gift that God had given him.

Bezaleel could have been very much like some laymen today. He could have said, "Look here, Lord, I want to wear these high priestly garments like Aaron. I want to serve You like that." But God said, "That is not the way I want you to serve me." In one sense this man's gift is more important than Aaron's gift. His gift was essential for the building of the tabernacle. God will give you a gift, friend, that will develop the talents that you have. God gives us talents, but He wants us to dedicate them to Him. Let's allow the Holy Spirit to take us and use us.

We do not all have the same talents and gifts. There is a wrong impression circulating in the church today that if you cannot sing in the choir, teach a Sunday school class, speak publicly, or be an usher, you are pretty much out of the picture. I think there are literally hundreds of gifts that God gives to men to serve Him. It is up to the individual to determine what is his gift. Whatever gift God has given you, He would like the Spirit of God to take it and use it for His service.

THE SABBATH DAY BECOMES A SIGN

There is something else in this chapter that is of profound interest and is important to see. It has to do with the Sabbath Day. It is something that many people pass over. The Sabbath Day was given to man right after creation, and it was observed universally. When we come to the Mosaic system, we find that God made it one of the Ten Commandments for the children of Israel. At this time God makes it quite clear that the Sabbath is *only* for the children of Israel.

And the Lord spake unto Moses, saying,

Speak thou also unto the children of Israel, saying, Verily my sabbaths ye shall keep: for it is a sign between me and you throughout your generations; that ye may know that I am the Lord that doth sanctify you [Exod. 31:12–13].

The Sabbath was given specifically to Israel. I do not believe it was ever given to the church. When someone asks me, "When was the Sabbath Day changed?" I always reply that it never was changed. It was done away with, as far as the church is concerned. We are not under the Sabbath Day which is Saturday. We do not observe Saturday—Jesus was dead that day and we are not serving a dead

Christ. On the first day of the week Jesus Christ rose from the dead. The church from the very beginning met on the first day of the week. That is when the church was born; the day of Pentecost was on the day *after* the Sabbath. The Sabbath was first given to the entire human race but man turned away from God, and God gave the Sabbath exclusively to Israel.

> **Ye shall keep the sabbath therefore; for it is holy unto you: every one that defileth it shall surely be put to death: for whosoever doeth any work therein, that soul shall be cut off from among his people [Exod. 31:14].**

I would like to ask the people who claim to keep the Sabbath if they keep it all the time. And are those of their number who do not keep the Sabbath all the time put to death as the law requires?

> **Six days may work be done; but in the seventh is the sabbath of rest, holy to the LORD: whosoever doeth any work in the sabbath day, he shall surely be put to death [Exod. 31:15].**

If a man was found gathering sticks on the Sabbath Day, he was stoned to death in Israel.

> **Wherefore the children of Israel shall keep the sabbath, to observe the sabbath throughout their generations, for a perpetual covenant.**

> **It is a sign between me and the children of Israel for ever: for in six days the LORD made heaven and earth, and on the seventh day he rested, and was refreshed [Exod. 31:16–17].**

This passage expressly says that the children of Israel, not the church, were to keep the Sabbath. The Israelites are an earthly people belonging to the first creation. The church is a new creation and it was given a new day to observe which is the first day of the week.

CHAPTER 32

THEME: *The golden calf; condemnation of Israel's apostasy; judgment; the intercession of Moses*

THE GOLDEN CALF

This chapter presents tragedy as far as the children of Israel are concerned, and yet it is here we see one of the greatest teachings and revelations concerning our God. Also, this is one of the greatest lessons on prayer found in the Bible.

> And when the people saw that Moses delayed to come down out of the mount, the people gathered themselves together unto Aaron, and said unto him, Up, make us gods, which shall go before us; for as for this Moses, the man that brought us up out of the land of Egypt, we wot not what is become of him [Exod. 32:1].

The word *wot* simply means we "know" not. The people thought Moses was gone, probably had been killed. Since he was gone, they wanted to make idols (gods) to lead them on the wilderness march. Right away they lapsed into idolatry. You would think Aaron, who was the high priest, would try to stop them, but he did not. Aaron went along with the liberalism of the people wanting to return to idolatry.

> And Aaron said unto them, Break off the golden earrings, which are in the ears of your wives, of your sons, and of your daughters, and bring them unto me [Exod. 32:2].

During that time earrings were a sign of idolatry (see Gen. 35:4). It was a sign that these people were serving the gods of Egypt. Now they were to bring these earrings to Aaron.

And all the people brake off the golden earrings which were in their ears, and brought them unto Aaron.

And he received them at their hand, and fashioned it with a graving tool, after he had made it a molten calf: and they said, These be thy gods, O Israel, which brought thee up out of the land of Egypt [Exod. 32:3-4].

Can you imagine these people lapsing into idolatry this quickly? It would be inconceivable to me if it were not for the fact that I have watched the church lapse into apostasy that I never dreamed I would live to see.

And they rose up early on the morrow, and offered burnt offerings, and brought peace offerings; and the people sat down to eat and to drink, and rose up to play [Exod. 32:6].

Gross immorality was involved here. They have already departed from God after they had told Him that they would keep all of His commandments. As you can see, they are not keeping any of them.

All this time Moses is on the mountain receiving the Law, the instructions; and the blueprint for the tabernacle.

CONDEMNATION OF ISRAEL'S APOSTASY

And the LORD said unto Moses, Go, get thee down; for thy people, which thou broughtest out of the land of Egypt, have corrupted themselves:

They have turned aside quickly out of the way which I commanded them: they have made them a molten calf, and have worshipped it, and have sacrificed thereunto, and said, These be thy gods, O Israel, which have brought thee up out of the land of Egypt [Exod. 32:7-8].

God did not redeem Israel because they were superior, greater, or better than any other nation. They were none of these things. God said, "I knew you were a stiffnecked people."

> **And the LORD said unto Moses, I have seen this people, and, behold, it is a stiffnecked people:**
>
> **Now therefore let me alone, that my wrath may wax hot against them, and that I may consume them: and I will make of thee a great nation [Exod. 32:9–10].**

This was a real temptation to Moses. God is saying, "Moses, I will use you like I used Abraham, and I will make of you a great nation, and I will still be able to make good my covenant with Abraham." Now notice what Moses does. He is an example of one of the greatest prayers in all of Scripture.

> **And Moses besought the LORD his God, and said, LORD, why doth thy wrath wax hot against thy people, which thou hast brought forth out of the land of Egypt with great power, and with a mighty hand? [Exod. 32:11].**

God asks Moses to "remember." God says, "Moses, get thee down, for *thy* people that *thou* hast brought forth out of the land of Egypt have corrupted themselves." Now Moses really talks back to God. (There is none of this pious piffle that you hear today in so many prayers. We have so much hypocrisy in some of our prayers that it is no wonder prayer meetings are dead. If we would talk honestly and frankly to God, prayer meeting would be the most exciting meeting in the church.) Listen to what Moses said, "Lord, I think You made a mistake. I do not recall bringing any people out of Egypt. And they are not *my* people; they are *Your* people. You brought them out of Egypt and You did it with a mighty hand. I could not bring them out. You have made a mistake, Lord." Can you imagine talking to God like that? Moses did!

Wherefore should the Egyptians speak, and say, For mischief did he bring them out, to slay them in the mountains, and to consume them from the face of the earth? Turn from thy fierce wrath and repent of this evil against thy people [Exod. 32:12].

Then Moses tells the Lord, "You brought Your people out of the land of Egypt, but suppose that You do not take them into the land. The Egyptians would say that You were able to lead them out of Egypt but not able to take them into the land. They are Your people, Lord. You promised to bring them into the land."

Next, Moses gives God a third reason for turning aside from His wrath against the Israelites.

Remember Abraham, Isaac, and Israel, thy servants, to whom thou swarest by thine own self, and saidst unto them, I will multiply your seed as the stars of heaven, and all this land that I have spoken of will I give unto your seed, and they shall inherit it for ever [Exod. 32:13].

Moses continues, "Lord, remember Abraham, Isaac, and Israel; You made a promise to them. You promised to multiply their seed and give them a land."

And the LORD repented of the evil which he thought to do unto his people [Exod. 32:14].

When Moses prayed like that, it moved the arm of God. If we were more honest in praying, we would see more answers—that is, more visible answers to our prayers. We always receive an answer to our prayers, but I think the Lord tells most of us no because we do not really pray honestly to Him.

JUDGMENT

And Moses turned, and went down from the mount, and the two tables of the testimony were in his hand: the tables were written on both their sides; on the one side and on the other were they written.

And the tables were the work of God, and the writing was the writing of God, graven upon the tables.

And when Joshua heard the noise of the people as they shouted, he said unto Moses. There is a noise of war in the camp.

And he said, It is not the voice of them that shout for mastery, neither is it the voice of them that cry for being overcome: but the noise of them that sing do I hear [Exod. 32:15–18].

The children of Israel were having a high old time, friends. They were worshiping their golden calf and living in sin.

And it came to pass, as soon as he came nigh unto the camp, that he saw the calf, and the dancing: and Moses' anger waxed hot, and he cast the tables out of his hands, and brake them beneath the mount.

And he took the calf which they had made, and burnt it in the fire, and ground it to powder, and strawed it upon the water, and made the children of Israel drink of it.

And Moses said unto Aaron, What did this people unto thee, that thou hast brought so great a sin upon them? [Exod. 32:19–21].

Now listen to Aaron try to crawfish out of it all. This would really be humorous, if it were not so serious a matter.

> And Aaron said, Let not the anger of my lord wax hot:
> thou knowest the people, that they are set on mischief.
>
> For they said unto me, Make us gods, which shall go
> before us: for as for this Moses, the man that brought us
> up out of the land of Egypt, we wot not what is become of
> him [Exod. 32:22–23].

In other words, Moses is getting the blame for what happened. The
children of Israel thought that Moses had deserted them, and so they
turned to the golden calf. Aaron continues:

> And I said unto them, Whosoever hath any gold, let
> them break it off. So they gave it me: then I cast it into
> the fire, and there came out this calf [Exod. 32:24].

You cannot help but laugh at Aaron's statement. I think Moses must
have laughed with incredulity. "You mean, Aaron, that you poured
gold into the fire and the calf walked out?" A few verses back we were
told, you remember, that Aaron fashioned the calf with tools. What
Aaron did was lie.

> And when Moses saw that the people were naked; (for
> Aaron had made them naked unto their shame among
> their enemies:) [Exod. 32:25].

This matter of nudism, sex, and dope is not new. I think you can look
at the Israelites in this instance and see the whole bit. Moses will see
this thing through. He is really angry. At the same time, however, notice what an intercessor he is for these people. He lays hold of the
heart of God and moves the hand of God.

It is time for Moses to move in with extreme surgery. When you
have cancer, and I know this from personal experience, you want to
try to get rid of it. If it means cutting away half of your body, you want
to get rid of it. Sin is an awful cancer, and God uses extreme surgery in
this case by slaying those who were guilty.

> Then Moses stood in the gate of the camp, and said,
> Who is on the LORD's side? let him come unto me. And
> all the sons of Levi gathered themselves together unto
> him.
>
> And he said unto them, Thus saith the LORD God of Is-
> rael, Put every man his sword by his side, and go in and
> out from gate to gate throughout the camp, and slay
> every man his brother, and every man his companion,
> and every man his neighbour [Exod. 32:26–27].

This judgment is serious and extreme. It had to be that because there had been terrible sin. Liberalism has crept into our churches, and we have allowed it to stay there unchecked. I can remember when I came before a church court to be examined for the ministry. A young fellow from a liberal seminary was also there to be examined. I have never seen anyone who knew as little theology and Bible as this boy, and what he did know he had all mixed up. It was clear that he had little knowledge and no faith. He could never even explain the great doctrines of the faith. In fact, one man very patiently said to him, "Well, if you don't believe it, at least you ought to know what you don't believe!" But he didn't. Then one old man who knew this boy's father, said, "This boy's father was a great preacher in the past. He was sound in the faith and I know that one day this boy will come around and will get straightened out." It was not unanimous but the council accepted him. It made me sick at heart to be brought in at the same time with a fellow who did not believe anything at all.

The way this council handled the situation is not the way Moses would have handled it! He would not have drawn a sword and slain the fellow, but he would not have accepted him as a preacher. He would have given that boy a Bible and told him to go to Bible school, learn a little Bible, and then come back and he could be examined again and see if he was fit for the ministry. Because of similar actions by other councils, liberalism has come into the organized church and has taken over. You cannot compromise with sin. Someone has said,

"Compromise is immoral," and it is especially immoral in the church. Moses did not do a very good job of compromising. He used extreme surgery.

And the children of Levi did according to the word of Moses: and there fell of the people that day about three thousand men [Exod. 32:28].

Those that were guilty were slain, and that cleaned up the camp pretty well. Many people are apt to say that this was brutal. Look at it this way. Was it better to cut out the cancer now and save the nation or let the cancer grow and destroy the nation? Think of the men, women, and children in the camp who were not guilty. If the men who had led Israel into idolatry had been allowed to live, the nation would never have entered the Promised Land. That, of course, is what is happening in the church in many places. I see church after church lose its importance and its influence and become useless because it allowed liberalism to creep in. We are soft and sentimental and silly. Sometimes we are even stupid in the way we handle evil.

THE INTERCESSION OF MOSES

And it came to pass on the morrow, that Moses said unto the people, Ye have sinned a great sin: and now I will go up unto the LORD; peradventure I shall make an atonement for your sin [Exod. 32:30].

An atonement *covered* up sin. That is the way sin was handled before Jesus Christ came to earth and died on the Cross. After the Cross, sin is removed. Now Moses gives his fourth reason for taking the children of Israel into the Promised Land.

And Moses returned unto the LORD, and said, Oh, this people have sinned a great sin, and have made them gods of gold [Exod. 32:31].

What is this? Confession. If you want to get along with God, you will have to agree with Him about sin. Sin is sin and it must be confessed. It does not matter who you are, either. These are God's chosen people, the children of Israel, and Moses says, "We have sinned!" Israel had sinned a great sin and made gods of gold. Moses spelled out the sin before God. And, friends, when we confess our sin to God, we should spell it out. Tell God exactly what it is.

> **Yet now, if thou wilt forgive their sin—; and if not, blot me, I pray thee, out of thy book which thou hast written [Exod. 32:32].**

Moses said, "I take my place with the people. I identify myself with them, and if You intend to blot them out, blot me out also." Remember that God had told Moses that He could still make good His covenant to Abraham, Isaac, and Jacob by simply making a nation from Moses. But Moses said, "No, I identify myself with the people. If You do not intend to bring them into the land, then blot me out with them." Notice that what moves the heart of God moves the hand of God.

> **And the LORD said unto Moses, Whosoever hath sinned against me, him will I blot out of my book [Exod. 32:33].**

God deals individually and personally with sin.

> **Therefore now go, lead the people unto the place of which I have spoken unto thee: behold, mine Angel shall go before thee: nevertheless in the day when I visit I will visit their sin upon them.**

> **And the LORD plagued the people, because they made the calf, which Aaron made [Exod. 32:34–35].**

God will deal with sin personally. He will, however, take the people into the land. Those that had not sinned in the idolatry of the calf would be led by the Angel of God. Now the Angel of the Lord in the Old Testament is the visible presence of Christ—the pre-incarnate Christ. Because of Moses' intercession, God has not given up on His people. This should impress upon us the extreme importance of prayer.

CHAPTER 33

THEME: *Israel's journey continues; the tabernacle is placed outside the camp; Moses' prayer and the Lord's answer*

ISRAEL'S JOURNEY CONTINUES

And the LORD said unto Moses, Depart, and go up hence, thou and the people which thou hast brought up out of the land of Egypt, unto the land which I sware unto Abraham, to Isaac, and to Jacob, saying, Unto thy seed will I give it:

And I will send an angel before thee; and I will drive out the Canaanite, the Amorite, and the Hittite, and the Perizzite, the Hivite, and the Jebusite [Exod. 33:1–2].

God is preparing Israel to enter the land. We will see them resume their wilderness march in the Book of Numbers. (The Book of Leviticus is the continuation of the instructions for the service of the tabernacle which they are just setting up in the Book of Exodus.)

Unto a land flowing with milk and honey: for I will not go up in the midst of thee: for thou art a stiffnecked people: lest I consume thee in the way.

And when the people heard these evil tidings, they mourned: and no man did put on him his ornaments [Exod. 33:3–4].

These ornaments, as we have already seen, were heathen. Their earrings, for example, demonstrated the fact that they were still worshiping the gods of Egypt. The earrings were a sign of it. This is very much like the wearing of a cross, although it is meaningless today as an identification of a Christian.

> **For the Lord had said unto Moses, Say unto the children of Israel, Ye are a stiffnecked people: I will come up into the midst of thee in a moment, and consume thee: therefore now put off thy ornaments from thee, that I may know what to do unto thee [Exod. 33:5].**

This is the third time God has called Israel a stiff-necked people. God is making it clear to them that He had not come to redeem His people because they were superior.

God asks them to remove the signs that show they are heathen and pagan and take a stand for God. I personally believe that is the reason that baptism (water baptism) was so important in the early church. It was an evidence that a person had left the old and was taking a stand for the new. This should give that type of testimony today. And so:

> **And the children of Israel stripped themselves of their ornaments by the mount Horeb [Exod. 33:6].**

THE TABERNACLE IS PLACED OUTSIDE THE CAMP

> **And Moses took the tabernacle, and pitched it without the camp, afar off from the camp, and called it the Tabernacle of the congregation. And it came to pass, that every one which sought the Lord went out unto the tabernacle of the congregation, which was without the camp [Exod. 33:7].**

As the tabernacle is being constructed, Moses has it set up without the camp, or outside the camp. The tabernacle at this point is only a tent of meeting. It was probably just a tent or maybe the outer fence that later enclosed the tabernacle.

Tabernacle Floor Plan

(West)

Holy
of Holies

Ark of the Covenant

Mercy Seat

Tabernacle Proper

Altar of Incense

Golden Lampstand

Table of Showbread

(South)

(North)

OUTER COURT

Laver

Brazen Altar

(East)

And it came to pass, when Moses went out unto the tabernacle, that all the people rose up, and stood every
man at his tent door, and looked after Moses, until he
was gone into the tabernacle.

And it came to pass, as Moses entered into the tabernacle, the cloudy pillar descended, and stood at the
door of the tabernacle, and the LORD talked with Moses
[Exod. 33:8–9].

The question arises, "Has anyone seen God?" John 1:18 tells us that
no man has seen God at any time. John 14:9 reveals that those who
have seen Jesus Christ have seen the Father. The Lord Jesus Christ is
the revelation of God veiled in human flesh. In the Old Testament one
of His names was "Angel of the Lord." It was the Angel of the Lord that
talked with Moses.

And the LORD spake unto Moses face to face, as a man
speaketh unto his friend [Exod. 33:11a].

Just as friends speak to each other face to face, God and Moses talked.
Yet Moses did not see God.

And he turned again into the camp: but his servant
Joshua, the son of Nun, a young man, departed not out
of the tabernacle [Exod. 33:11b].

Once again Joshua is mentioned. He is the man God is preparing to
succeed Moses. I do not think that anyone suspected it at the time, but
when we get to the Book of Joshua, we will see that he was probably
the most unlikely person of all to succeed Moses.

MOSES' PRAYER AND THE LORD'S ANSWER

And Moses said unto the LORD, See, thou sayest unto me,
Bring up this people: and thou hast not let me know
whom thou wilt send with me. Yet thou hast said, I

> know thee by name, and thou hast also found grace in
> my sight.
>
> Now therefore, I pray thee, if I have found grace in thy
> sight, shew me now thy way, that I may know thee, that I
> may find grace in thy sight: and consider that this na-
> tion is thy people [Exod. 33:12–13].

Moses was asking for the same thing that Paul did in Philippians
3:10, "That I may know him. . . ." It is the same thing that Philip
meant when in John 14:8 he said, ". . . shew us the Father, and it sufficeth us." I believe every sincere child of God has a desire to know God.

> And he said, My presence shall go with thee, and I will
> give thee rest.
>
> And he said unto him, If thy presence go not with me,
> carry us not up hence [Exod. 33:14–15].

Moses knew that he needed the presence of God with him. He knew
that he could not make it on his own.

> For wherein shall it be known here that I and thy people
> have found grace in thy sight? is it not in that thou goest
> with us? so shall we be separated, I and thy people,
> from all the people that are upon the face of the earth
> [Exod. 33:16].

It is important to notice that God made the Israelites a peculiar people
for a very definite reason. The church is also to be a peculiar people
today. This means we are to be a people for God; it does not mean that
we are to be oddballs.

> And the LORD said unto Moses, I will do this thing also
> that thou hast spoken: for thou hast found grace in my
> sight, and I know thee by name [Exod. 33:17].

Moses is becoming very intimate with God.

> **And he said, I beseech thee, shew me thy glory [Exod.
> 33:18].**

Moses could not actually *see* God face to face.

> **And he said, I will make all my goodness pass before
> thee, and I will proclaim the name of the LORD before
> thee: and will be gracious to whom I will be gracious,
> and will shew mercy on whom I will shew mercy [Exod.
> 33:19].**

Paul uses this verse in Romans 9:15 when he says, "For he saith to
Moses, I will have mercy on whom I will have mercy, and I will have
compassion on whom I will have compassion."

> **And he said, Thou canst not see my face: for there shall
> no man see me, and live [Exod. 33:20].**

It is a fact, friend, you are *not* going to see God face to face.

> **And the LORD said, Behold, there is a place by me, and
> thou shalt stand upon a rock:**
>
> **And it shall come to pass, while my glory passeth by,
> that I will put thee in a clift of the rock, and will cover
> thee with my hand while I pass by:**
>
> **And I will take away mine hand, and thou shalt see my
> back parts: but my face shall not be seen [Exod. 33:21–
> 23].**

This passage is speaking about the glory being a representation of
God. The Lord Jesus said that when He comes the second time, there
would be the sign of the Son of man in heaven. Matthew 24:30 states:

"And then shall appear the sign of the Son of man in heaven: and then shall all the tribes of the earth mourn, and they shall see the Son of man coming in the clouds of heaven with power and great glory." I think that sign is the Shekinah glory spoken of in Exodus 33:21–23. When Christ took upon Himself human flesh, the glory was not there. He took a humble place and put aside His glory, but He was still God. That is why He could say, "He that hath seen me hath seen the Father."

We are not going to see God. We will see the Lord Jesus Christ, and He will be in human form because that is the form He took here on earth. Today He is in a glorified body, and someday we shall be like Him we are told in 1 John 3:2 which says, "Beloved, now are we the sons of God, and it doth not yet appear what we shall be: but we know that, when he shall appear, we shall be like him; for we shall see him as he is." This is the anticipation and hope of believers who are walking by faith. That is the way Moses is going to walk. He knew that God's presence had to go with him or failure would be the result.

We need His presence today also to face the problems of everyday life.

CHAPTER 34

THEME: The tables of the Law renewed; Moses' commission is renewed; Moses' face shines

THE TABLES OF THE LAW RENEWED

And the Lᴏʀᴅ said unto Moses, Hew thee two tables of stone like unto the first: and I will write upon these tables the words that were in the first tables, which thou brakest.

And be ready in the morning, and come up in the morning unto mount Sinai, and present thyself there to me in the top of the mount.

And no man shall come up with thee, neither let any man be seen throughout all the mount; neither let the flocks nor herds feed before that mount.

And he hewed two tables of stone like unto the first; and Moses rose up early in the morning, and went up unto mount Sinai, as the Lᴏʀᴅ had commanded him, and took in his hand the two tables of stone [Exod. 34:1–4].

These are the second tables of the Law. The first tables were broken by Moses when he descended Mount Sinai and found that the children of Israel had made a golden calf and were worshiping it. He now comes back to the mount with blank tables of stone.

And the Lᴏʀᴅ descended in the cloud, and stood with him there, and proclaimed the name of the Lᴏʀᴅ [Exod. 34:5].

The Lord is now proclaiming His name. This is a tremendous advance for both Moses and the children of Israel. A name has meaning. When you hear the name Caesar, what do you think of? When you hear the

name Abraham Lincoln, what do you think of? You conjure up certain
images in your mind. God is now proclaiming His name and He
wants the Israelites to remember their experiences with Him since
they left the land of Egypt.

> **And the Lᴏʀᴅ passed by before him, and proclaimed,**
> **The Lᴏʀᴅ, The Lᴏʀᴅ God, merciful and gracious,**
> **longsuffering, and abundant in goodness and truth,**
>
> **Keeping mercy for thousands, forgiving iniquity and**
> **transgression and sin, and that will by no means clear**
> **the guilty [Exod. 34:6–7a].**

God does not extend mercy by shutting His eyes to the guilty or by
saying, "I will just forget that sin." Sin must be punished and a penalty must be paid. God by no means clears the guilty. What happens
then? How does He keep His mercy and take care of iniquity at the
same time? A sacrifice has been provided. The sacrifices Israel made
in that day did not *take away* sin but they pointed to that "Perfect
Sacrifice," the Lord Jesus Christ, who, when He did come, put away
sin by His death on the Cross.

> **visiting the iniquity of the fathers upon the children,**
> **and upon the children's children, unto the third and to**
> **the fourth generation [Exod. 34:7b].**

It is a good thing to remember that today you can commit a sin that
will affect your children, your grandchildren, your great-grand-
children, and your great-great-grandchildren.

I took a certain course in abnormal psychology in college—
psychology was my second major. I almost accepted a scholarship to
go on with my studies in this field. One day we went on a tour of a
mental hospital in Bolivar, Tennessee. We were shown different forms
of abnormality. All of the patients were suffering from one mental disease or another. After we had seen one particular group, a member of
our class asked the doctor what caused these diseases. The doctor

simply replied, "It was either the sins of the father or the grandfather, or it could have been the sins of the great-grandfather."

A doctor in Nashville took me to the hospital one morning where he was going to operate on some blind children, although it would give them only partial sight. "What made them blind?" I asked. He replied, "It was the sins of their fathers." Believe me, friend, you cannot break His laws with impunity. God is always the same. His laws do not change. But thank God "He keeps mercy for thousands, forgiving iniquity." If we only turn to Him, we will find mercy.

And Moses made haste, and bowed his head toward the earth, and worshipped.

And he said, If now I have found grace in thy sight, O LORD, let my LORD, I pray thee, go among us; for it is a stiffnecked people; and pardon our iniquity and our sin, and take us for thine inheritance [Exod. 34:8–9].

This is about the fourth time these people have been called stiffnecked. I hope by this time that you realize God never saved the nation Israel because they were superior, or because they were doing so well, or because they promised to do good. They are a stiff-necked people.

MOSES' COMMISSION IS RENEWED

And he said, Behold, I make a covenant: before all thy people I will do marvels, such as have not been done in all the earth, nor in any nation: and all the people among which thou art shall see the work of the LORD: for it is a terrible thing that I will do with thee [Exod. 34:10].

The word terrible means "to incite terror." This word does not have the same meaning as we give to terrible. It was part of the shield of God that He was putting around His people. They would have been devoured by the enemy if He had not done this.

> Observe thou that which I command thee this day: be-
> hold, I drive out before thee the Amorite, and the Ca-
> naanite, and the Hittite, and the Perizzite, and the
> Hivite, and the Jebusite [Exod. 34:11].

God says that He will drive out all of their enemies, and this is the
third time He has mentioned this.

> Take heed to thyself, lest thou make a covenant with the
> inhabitants of the land whither thou goest, lest it be for a
> snare in the midst of thee [Exod. 34:12].

God warned them not to make a covenant with any of the people of the
land. When the Gibeonites came to Joshua (in the Book of Joshua),
they tricked the Israelites. They pretended that they had come from
afar and had old stale bread to prove it—to Joshua, at least. Why didn't
God want Israel to make covenants with the people in the land of Canaan? If they made any covenants with these people, it would become
a snare to them and lead them back into idolatry.

> But ye shall destroy their altars, break their images,
> and cut down their groves:
>
> For thou shalt worship no other god: for the LORD, whose
> name is Jealous, is a jealous God [Exod. 34:13–14].

He is a jealous God and does not want to share His honor and glory
with false gods. There is no reason to apologize for God's being jealous either. I once heard a wife say, "My husband is not jealous of me."
She was boasting of that fact. But I could have told her that if her
husband was not jealous, he did not love her. Anything or any person
you love, you are jealous of, and do not like to share with others. You
can be jealous in an evil way, but this is not what we are talking about.
When you love a person, you have a concern and you care for them.

Lest thou make a covenant with the inhabitants of the
land, and they go a-whoring after their gods, and do
sacrifice unto their gods, and one call thee, and thou eat
of his sacrifice;

And thou take of their daughters unto thy sons, and
their daughters go a-whoring after their gods, and make
thy sons go a-whoring after their gods.

Thou shalt make thee no molten gods [Exod. 34:15–17].

The land of Canaan was covered with idolatry just like a dog is covered with fleas. The land was filled with gross immorality, and God is warning Israel to keep herself separate from people engaged in these activities and make no covenant with them at all. Israel was to either destroy them or drive them out of the land. The critics down through the years have decried this. Apparently they have not investigated the reason for this extreme measure. Of course the obvious reason is that God was protecting His own from the horror of idolatry. But there is another reason. It is known today that venereal disease was in epidemic proportions among the inhabitants of Canaan. God was attempting to protect His people from the ravages of disease. Israel disobeyed God and did not completely clear the land of these people and suffered the sad consequences. Finally God sent Israel, disobedient and corrupt, into Babylonian captivity.

The feast of unleavened bread shalt thou keep. Seven
days thou shalt eat unleavened bread, as I commanded
thee, in the time of the month Abib: for in the month
Abib thou camest out from Egypt [Exod. 34:18].

God is preparing Israel to enter the land by reestablishing the feasts and sabbaths.

Thrice in the year shall all your menchildren appear before the Lord GOD, the God of Israel [Exod. 34:23].

God then goes on and gives many details concerning different things that the children of Israel were to do and were not to do.

> **Thou shalt not offer the blood of my sacrifice with leaven; neither shall the sacrifice of the feast of the passover be left unto the morning.**
>
> **The first of the firstfruits of thy land thou shalt bring unto the house of the LORD thy God. Thou shalt not seethe a kid in his mother's milk [Exod. 34:25–26].**

The Israelites were to put God *first!* To "seethe a kid" means, of course, to boil it. It is not to be boiled in its mother's milk. That is, they were to avoid doing the unnatural thing.

MOSES' FACE SHINES

> **And it came to pass, when Moses came down from mount Sinai with the two tables of testimony in Moses' hand, when he came down from the mount, that Moses wist not that the skin of his face shone while he talked with him.**
>
> **And when Aaron and all the children of Israel saw Moses, behold, the skin of his face shone; and they were afraid to come nigh him.**
>
> **And Moses called unto them; and Aaron and all the rulers of the congregation returned unto him: and Moses talked with them.**
>
> **And afterward all the children of Israel came nigh: and he gave them in commandment all that the LORD had spoken with him in mount Sinai.**
>
> **And till Moses had done speaking with them, he put a veil on his face.**

But when Moses went in before the LORD to speak with him, he took the veil off, until he came out. And he came out, and spake unto the children of Israel that which he was commanded.

And the children of Israel saw the face of Moses, that the skin of Moses' face shone: and Moses put the veil upon his face again, until he went in to speak with him [Exod. 34:29–35].

CHAPTER 35

THEME: The Sabbath reemphasized; free gifts for the tabernacle; Bezaleel and Aholiab called to the work

THE SABBATH REEMPHASIZED

In this chapter the Lord returns to talk to Israel about the Sabbath Day. This is the third time.

> And Moses gathered all the congregation of the children of Israel together, and said unto them, These are the words which the Lord hath commanded, that ye should do them.

> Six days shall work be done, but on the seventh day there shall be to you an holy day, a sabbath of rest to the Lord: whosoever doeth work therein shall be put to death.

> Ye shall kindle no fire throughout your habitations upon the sabbath day [Exod. 35:1–3].

The Lord insists that the first reason for the Sabbath is that it belongs to the first creation. God rested on the Sabbath Day. As mankind left the creative hand of God, he began to wander away from God. There came the day when mankind as a whole no longer recognized God but began to worship the creature. And man gave up keeping the Sabbath Day. Now God said that the Sabbath was a peculiar sign between Himself and the children of Israel. God began to lay down rules that actually apply more to Israel in the Promised Land than to any other place. If anyone did work on the Sabbath Day, he was stoned to death. It would be very hard to carry on our society without someone working on the Sabbath Day, which is Saturday. Suppose no fire was kindled on the Sabbath. This would cause great problems in the frozen North. God's laws were made to suit the land in which Israel lived.

FREE GIFTS FOR THE TABERNACLE

And Moses spake unto all the congregation of the children of Israel, saying, This is the thing which the Lord
commanded, saying,

Take ye from among you an offering unto the Lord: whosoever is of a willing heart, let him bring it, an offering
of the Lord; gold, and silver, and brass [Exod. 35:4–5].

These gifts for the making of the tabernacle were to be voluntary. The
people were not required to bring anything. There was no demand put
upon them at all. This is not the tithe. This is a voluntary gift. They
were to bring other things besides the gold, silver, and brass, as we
shall see.

And blue, and purple, and scarlet, and fine linen, and
goats' hair.

And rams' skins dyed red, and badgers' skins, and shittim wood,

And oil for the light, and spices for anointing oil, and
for the sweet incense,

And onyx stones, and stones to be set for the ephod, and
for the breastplate [Exod. 35:6–9].

These are the different things that the children of Israel could give to
the building of the tabernacle. In that day there was no such thing as
legal tender. The method of barter was the exchange of goods; so the
Israelites were giving things rather than money to the Lord's work.

This is still a way people can serve the Lord. Several years ago in
San Diego a man donated two ampex recorders to our radio ministry.
These recorders were very valuable and came to us at the time when
we were really in need of them. Many people think that you have to
always write out a check—do not misunderstand, we need money

too—but the Lord can also be served when you donate things to His service.

The question is repeatedly asked, "Where did the children of Israel get the different articles they gave to the tabernacle when they had been *slaves* in Egypt?" Remember that God said that they would come out of Egypt with great wealth (Gen. 15:14). He made sure they collected their back wages. The Egyptians were so glad to rid the land of the Israelites that they gave them whatever they asked. So Israel left with a great deal of the wealth of Egypt.

BEZALEEL AND AHOLIAB CALLED TO THE WORK

And Moses said unto the children of Israel, See, the LORD hath called by name Bezaleel the son of Uri, the son of Hur, of the tribe of Judah;

And he hath filled him with the spirit of God, in wisdom, in understanding, and in knowledge, and in all manner of workmanship [Exod. 35:30–31].

Bezaleel is the man God equipped to make the articles of furniture that are so important in the tabernacle.

And he hath put in his heart that he may teach, both he, and Aholiab, the son of Ahisamach, of the tribe of Dan [Exod. 35:34].

God gave Bezaleel the ability to pass on his gift to others.

Them hath he filled with wisdom of heart, to work all manner of work, of the engraver, and of the cunning workman, and of the embroiderer, in blue, and in purple, in scarlet, and in fine linen, and of the weaver, even of them that do any work, and of those that devise cunning work [Exod. 35:35].

The tabernacle was a beautiful object. It was a jewel in the desert. It was not large, not a great warehouse, only a small building. It has been estimated that about five million dollars went into the construction of the tabernacle according to the value of the metals of a few years ago. The value in inflationary times would even be greater. The tabernacle was God's precious jewel; a picture of His Son, Jesus Christ.

The tabernacle erected, and the tents of Israel around it.

CHAPTER 36

THEME: Construction of the tabernacle

This chapter returns us to the tabernacle. We have already seen the instructions regarding how to build it. Now we see they are building it according to instructions. Following the blueprint is very important because the tabernacle is God's portrait of Christ. It reveals Him.

> **Then wrought Bezaleel and Aholiab, and every wise-hearted man, in whom the LORD put wisdom and understanding to know how to work all manner of work for the service of the sanctuary, according to all that the LORD had commanded [Exod. 36:1].**

Every member of the crew, which was probably a large number of folk, was engaged in the building of the tabernacle with the wisdom and understanding God had given him. The man in charge was Bezaleel.

> **And Moses called Bezaleel and Aholiab, and every wise-hearted man, in whose heart the LORD had put wisdom, even every one whose heart stirred him up to come unto the work to do it! [Exod. 36:2].**

Now notice something here that is very important and essential in the work of the Lord. If you are serving the Lord grudgingly, do not do it. God cannot use this kind of an attitude. Building the tabernacle are men who are carving out beautiful articles of furniture that are to be used in the worship of the Lord. This is not a "job" to them. They are not watching the clock. They do not belong to a union. They do not just work a certain number of hours a week and quit. They are not building the tabernacle because it is their duty. They are not working because they have to work. They have been slaves in the past and here they are slaving again, but this time because they want to. Their hearts are in their work. That is the way you are to do God's work.

A young preacher once told me, "I like the ministry but I do not like preaching." I suggested he get out of the ministry. The ministry is no place for a man who does not *love* to study and preach the Word of God. If a preacher cannot do his job with enthusiasm and preach with enthusiasm, he should not be in the ministry.

I once listened to a former student of mine preach. What a hassle, what an effort, what a lack of enthusiasm! My friend, if you cannot preach or serve the Lord with verve, vigor, and vitality, don't do it at all. God doesn't want people in His service who would rather be doing something else.

Notice Bezaleel rushing at top speed. Is he going to a football game, a baseball game, or some social? No! Bezaleel is going to work—work for the Lord. You know, if people came to church next Sunday filled with enthusiasm, the whole town would soon be coming out to see what in the world was happening in the church. It would be a revival. God's work is to be done with joy and happiness. We are to serve Him with gladness. In Romans 14:5 the apostle Paul said, ". . . Let every man be fully persuaded in his own mind." This is how we are to serve the Lord. We are to be fully persuaded that we are serving Him because we want to and because we are eager to please Him. Again, in 1 Corinthians 9:16 Paul tells us, ". . . woe is unto me, if I preach not the gospel!" Paul *wanted* to preach the gospel.

Those three hundred men of Gideon that went down to the water did not lean over the edge and lap it up. They dipped their hands in the water and brought it up to their mouths, watching for the enemy. They said, "Where are those Midianites? We want to get them." This account is found in Judges 7:5–7. This is the kind of enthusiasm we need in the church today. We are bogged down with too many dead saints, and I mean they are dead before they are buried.

And they received of Moses all the offering, which the children of Israel had brought for the work of the service

of the sanctuary, to make it withal. And they brought yet
unto him free offerings every morning.

And all the wise men, that wrought all the work of the
sanctuary, came every man from his work which they
made:

And they spake unto Moses, saying, The people bring
much more than enough for the service of the work,
which the LORD commanded to make [Exod. 36:3–5].

This is the only place on record, that I know of, where the people had
to be asked to stop giving. They brought a great deal more than was
needed to build and furnish the tabernacle. I have never seen an offering like this in my ministry! Nor have I ever heard of an offering like
this before or after.

And Moses gave commandment, and they caused it to be
proclaimed throughout the camp, saying, Let neither
man nor woman make any more work for the offering of
the sanctuary. So the people were restrained from
bringing [Exod. 36:6].

The people are urged not to give, and they have to be restrained and
told that they have brought enough. This is really amazing in the light
of the fact that these people were fresh out of slavery. They had never
owned anything before and now that they had riches you would think
they would not be so willing to give it away. But they give liberally,
joyfully, and enthusiastically to their God. Whatever you do for God,
this is the way you should do it. That is the way God wants it done.
    God wants us to give joyfully. There was a motto years ago that
said, "Give 'til it hurts." God says, "If it hurts, don't give." Our worship of God should be with joy, and so should our giving.
    It seems in this chapter that we are going over the different articles
and part of the tabernacle again. It sounds like repetition, but before
we were given the blueprint for the tabernacle, and now we come to

the execution of the job. We not only need a blueprint and materials, but we need to go to work. The people of Israel are beginning the work in this chapter.

And every wise-hearted man among them that wrought the work of the tabernacle made ten curtains of fine twined linen, and blue, and purple, and scarlet: with cherubims of cunning work made he them [Exod. 36:8].

This was the covering of all the tabernacle. It was the covering that went first on the articles of furniture when they went out on the wilderness march. It was the fence outside. This fine twined Egyptian linen speaks of the righteousness of Christ. It speaks of His character and His work. It speaks of the righteousness that He provides for us so that we might be clothed to stand in God's presence. The important thing to notice is that Christ is adequate to meet our needs. He is able to save us. He is able to deliver us. He is able to keep us.

The curtains of goats' hair, the covering of rams' skins, and the boards and sockets also speak of the person of Christ in one way or another. Now the tabernacle was thirty cubits long by ten cubits wide by ten cubits high. It was made of acacia wood, and the boards were overlaid with gold all the way around. The boards were one and one-half cubits wide. On the wilderness march they were very heavy to carry and were carried in wagons. (However all of the articles of furniture were carried on the shoulders of the priests of the tribe of Levi.) The golden boards were to be placed upright but each one had certain sockets that fitted down into sockets of silver, and the entire tabernacle rested upon silver—silver typifies redemption. The tabernacle was held together by bars. Certain rings were put in each board, and when it was set up, these bars slipped through the rings and bound the tabernacle together. It was a very compact building.

The tabernacle had an inner veil that separated the main tabernacle into two compartments; the smaller compartment was called the Holy of Holies and the larger compartment was called the Holy Place. Everything in the tabernacle pictured some part of the person or work of the Lord Jesus Christ.

CHAPTER 37

THEME: The plan of the tabernacle

Everything mentioned in this chapter has been dealt with in previous chapters in the Book of Exodus. Rather than repeating the Scriptures which have been quoted in previous chapters, I will recap some of the highlights and the things which I feel are of primary importance.

The two articles of furniture in the outer court were the brazen altar and the laver. When you stepped inside the Holy Place, there were three articles of furniture: the golden lampstand, the table of showbread, and the altar of incense. In the Holy of Holies was the ark of the covenant and the mercy seat.

There were three compartments to the tabernacle. And there were three entrances to the tabernacle. (1) There was a gate through the linen fence that surrounded the tabernacle. (2) There was an entrance which led into the Holy Place. (3) The third entrance led into the Holy of Holies, where only the high priest went once a year on the great Day of Atonement (as we shall see in Leviticus) and sprinkled blood on the mercy seat—which is what made it a *mercy* seat.

There were seven articles of furniture arranged in such a way as to give us a wonderful picture. The brazen altar speaks of the Cross of Christ where we receive forgiveness of sin. The laver speaks of the fact that Christ washes or cleanses those who are His own. The laver is where we confess our sins, and receive His forgiveness and cleansing.

The Holy Place is the place of worship. In it is the golden lampstand typifying Christ, the Light of the World. The table of showbread pictures Christ as the Bread of Life upon which we feed. The altar of incense is the place of prayer. It speaks of the fact that Christ is our Intercessor. In the Epistle to the Hebrews the altar of incense is placed in the Holy of Holies (rather than in the Holy Place) because our Intercessor is now in heaven. But the altar of incense is outside in the Holy

The artist, George Howell, has sketched the tabernacle interior without the separating veil. The rear compartment shows the Holy of Holies which housed the ark of the covenant. The front compartment pictures the Holy Place in which were the lampstand, the altar of incense, and the table of showbread.

Place also where you and I can come today. When believers want to worship God, they come into the Holy Place. Confession, praise, thanksgiving, intercession, making requests—these are the things that have to do with worship. And all of this is in the Holy Place. If you want the light which the world gives, you go outside, but if you want light from the lampstand, you must come inside. In order to serve Christ you cannot walk by the wisdom of the world but by the light of the Word of God.

The Holy of Holies pictures Jesus Christ in the presence of God. In the Book of Hebrews we are told to come to the throne of grace. The mercy seat pictures this, and this is where we find grace to help and mercy in time of need. There is a mercy seat for believers in heaven.

When Christ came to earth, He not only fulfilled the picture of the tabernacle, He did something quite unusual. The tabernacle in the wilderness was always horizontal with the earth. It was set up on the flat surface of the ground, with its pillars and boards fitting into the sockets they put down. But when Christ came to pay the price for our sins, He made the tabernacle perpendicular. The Cross was the brazen altar where the Lamb of God was offered for our sins. He died down here to save us. But He returned to heaven where He lives today to keep us saved. The Holy of Holies is in heaven today. We do not go horizontally to God by going to a building or to a man, but we look to heaven and go directly to Him—through Jesus Christ. "For there is one God, and one mediator between God and men, the man Christ Jesus" (1 Tim. 2:5).

Where are you today, friend, in relation to the tabernacle? Do you need to stand at the brazen altar and be saved? There are many folk—even church members—who need to go there. Are you a soiled Christian who needs to confess your sins at the laver and be cleansed? Or are you walking in darkness today? Step inside the Holy Place and walk by the light of the golden lampstand. Maybe your spiritual life is a little anemic, and you need to feed on the Bread of Life to gain nourishment. Maybe your prayer life is beggarly and you need to stand before the altar of incense. Perhaps you are in trouble and you need mercy, grace, and help. Well, there is a mercy seat for you today. Go there and accept the help that is waiting for you. God wants to bless and guide you.

CHAPTER 38

THEME: The plan of the tabernacle—continued

W e are still looking at the tabernacle in this chapter. Beginning at chapter 25, the blueprint for the tabernacle was given in every detail. Now Bezaleel and his helpers are constructing the building. In fact, by chapter 38 the tabernacle has been constructed, as I understand it, but has not yet been set in order. This chapter pays particular attention to the outer court.

As we shall see in the Book of Numbers, Israel traveled when the pillar of cloud started moving. The ark on the shoulders of the priests led the procession. When the cloud rested, Israel set up camp. The ark was put down on the desert sand and the tabernacle was set up around it. The siding of the gold-covered boards was put in place around it, the bars were slipped through the rings of the boards, and that bound the tabernacle together. Then over the boards were placed four coverings; the linen, goats' skins dyed red, the rams' skins, and the badger or sealskins for protection. The beauty of the tabernacle had to be seen from within. Everything in it spoke of worship, praise, adoration to God, and blessing to the individual.

The outer court, enclosed by the linen fence, was one hundred cubits by fifty cubits and contained the brazen altar and laver. This is where the sin questions was settled. The sinner would come to the gate and stand there as a sinner. The priest would lead him into the outer court. The sinner would put his right hand upon the head of the animal he had brought—whether it be lamb, goat, or ox. Then the animal was slain and the priest would offer it on the altar. That was as far as the individual went; from then on he went in the person of his priest. The priest had to stop at the laver and wash so that he could enter the Holy Place. In the Holy Place were three articles of furniture: the golden lampstand, the table of showbread, and the altar of incense, all of which spoke of worship. Next came the veil which separated the Holy Place from the Holy of Holies, and the priest did not dare go beyond that. He did not go into the Holy of Holies, where were the ark of the covenant and the mercy seat, because only the high priest entered this room and only once a year in behalf of the nation.

> **And he made the altar of burnt offering of shittim wood: five cubits was the length thereof, and five cubits the breadth thereof; it was foursquare; and three cubits the height thereof [Exod. 38:1].**

On the brazen altar the victim was offered and sin was judged. It was here the individual or the nation came to take care of the sin problem. When this altar was constructed, no other altar could be made. This was *the* approach to God and any other altar built anywhere else would have been blasphemy. It was in the place of prominence because the sin question was settled here. There could be no such thing as worship or blessing until one had come to the brazen altar.

The horns on the altar speak of strength—the ability of Jesus Christ to save. There are many instructions and details about the approach and care of this altar. There had to be certain pots, pans, staves and rings, etc. The important thing to remember, however, is its function of settling the sin problem.

> **And he made the laver of brass, and the foot of it of brass, of the lookingglasses of the women assembling, which assembled at the door of the tabernacle of the congregation [Exod. 38:8].**

The mirrors spoken of here were made of brass which was highly polished. Women have not changed; they carried mirrors in that day, too. The laver was made from these mirrors. The mirror represents the Word of God. It is the Bible that shows the believer his need for cleansing. The laver was there for cleansing. We have the same thing in our bathrooms today. We have a mirror, and beneath the mirror is a wash basin. The mirror does not wash the dirt off, and neither can the Law save you. You can rub up against it all you want to but the dirt remains. However, "there is a fountain filled with blood, drawn from

Immanuel's veins, and sinners plunged beneath that flood lose all their guilty stains."

> **And he made the court: on the south side southward the hangings of the court were of fine twined linen, an hundred cubits:**
>
> **Their pillars were twenty, and their brasen sockets twenty; the hooks of the pillars and their fillets were of silver.**
>
> **And for the north side the hangings were an hundred cubits, their pillars were twenty, and their sockets of brass twenty; the hooks of the pillars and their fillets of silver [Exod. 38:9–11].**

The fine twined linen speaks of the humanity of Christ, and it actually separated man from God.

I was greatly disturbed at this Easter season when someone handed me an article concerning a message that a so-called conservative president of a seminary gave at one of these "knife and fork" clubs. I had spoken at this club years ago. It was reported that this preacher said that all we had to do was follow the teachings of Jesus and peace would come to the world—even if you denied the deity of Christ. Well, that just is not true. There can be no peace for man apart from the shed blood of Christ. That linen fence, which pictured the humanity of Christ, shut man out from God. The *life* of Christ does not save us; it condemns us! It is the death of Christ that saves us. When we have preachers that pretend to be conservative giving a message like that, no wonder there is so much confusion in the world today! The Word of God, and especially the tabernacle, is like a picture book. If you just look at the picture you can understand that the life and teachings of Christ cannot save you. To begin with, you could not measure up to His life or His teachings. Nonsense to the contrary has been ground out by liberalism for years and has gotten us into the difficulty we are in today. It is time that someone puts it right on the line and tells the truth. The teachings of Christ cannot save you, friends. The death of Christ on the Cross saves you. That is the reason the brazen altar was there. The white linen fence shut out man from God, and God from man. Although the sockets for the tabernacle proper were silver, the sockets for the fence were brass. Brass, as we have already seen, is the metal of judgment. The picture of Christ in Revelation 1:15 speaks of his feet like "fine brass." I tell you, friend, that sin has to be judged. Man must recognize that he is a sinner. He cannot come into God's presence until the sin question is settled.

The hooks of the pillars and the fillets were of silver, however, and silver is the metal of redemption. The fence of the outer court kept man out, but God made a way for him to enter. He found a way to judge sin and provided a redemption for man that he might be clothed in the righteousness of Christ. What a picture! You can look at the tabernacle and get the gospel. God has given it to us in picture form.

There was an entrance to the court. Man did not climb over the fence. He had to come in through the gate.

And the hanging for the gate of the court was needlework, of blue, and purple, and scarlet, and fine twined linen: and twenty cubits was the length, and the height in the breadth was five cubits, answerable to the hangings of the court [Exod. 38:18].

All of the material and color speaks of the person of Christ. We have been through this before, but it will not hurt to repeat. Blue speaks of the fact that He came from heaven as deity. The scarlet speaks of His humanity and the blood He shed for mankind. The blue and scarlet combined make purple which speaks of His royalty. He was born King of the Jews.

The gate was as high as the fence was on the outside. It was about seven and one-half feet and that would be pretty hard even for a basketball player to look over. There was no way to get into the court except through this entrance. It was a wide entrance, wide enough for any sinner to enter, but it was the *only* way one could enter. Christ has said that He is the *way*, the *truth*, and the *life*. I like to think of the gate into the court as being the *way*.

The next of the three entrances that would bring one into the very presence of God, is the entrance into the Holy Place. I like to think of that as being "the truth." Christ also said that if you are going to worship God, you will have to worship Him in spirit and in *truth*. I do not mean to be harsh, but "worship" in a church that denies who Christ is and what He has done is not true worship. You have to worship Him in truth. You cannot deny the deity of Christ and the fact that He died for you and still worship Him. It would be best for a lot of people if they did not go to church (that is, to certain churches) at all. Their own condition is not good, and the church they are attending is insulting the Lord Jesus Christ by denying His deity.

Then the final entrance which brought one into the very Holy of Holies was the entrance through the veil which speaks of the life Christ gave up on the Cross. When He died, that veil was torn in two from the top to the bottom, signifying that the way to God was now open. That is *life*. Christ is the *way*, the *truth*, and the *life*. No one comes into the presence of the Father but by Him (John 14:6).

Next I want to call your attention to the question of the individual Israelite. The nation Israel is called a "son." God never called the individual Israelite, son. The question was, and is today, "Who is a Jew?" Is a Jew one who has been born a Jew or does his religion make him a Jew? In the Old Testament you had to be born a Jew to be one. And God made a provision that everyone had to be redeemed, which means that each individual had to be a born again one. Israel was a chosen nation, but each individual had to be redeemed.

And the silver of them that were numbered of the congregation was an hundred talents, and a thousand seven hundred and threescore and fifteen shekels, after the shekel of the sanctuary:

A bekah for every man, that is, half a shekel, after the shekel of the sanctuary, for every one that went to be numbered, from twenty years old and upward, for six hundred thousand and three thousand and five hundred and fifty men [Exod. 38:25–26].

The Jews brought silver because it was the metal of redemption. Every Israelite had to be redeemed to be acceptable. We have been redeemed by the precious blood of Christ which is more precious than silver or gold. Now, every individual Israelite was not saved. Only a remnant of the nation was saved, just as not all church members are saved.

A very small percentage of church members today are saved. A wealthy man in Tulsa, Oklahoma told me that for a long time he and his wife "played" church. "We sat down with the rest of the hypocrites. None of us were born again; we just put up a front. Before the sun went down we were all drunk." Being a church member doesn't mean very much in these days in which we live. You have to be redeemed. And the children of Israel had to be redeemed.

And of the hundred talents of silver were cast the sockets of the sanctuary, and the sockets of the veil; an hundred sockets of the hundred talents, a talent for a socket [Exod. 38:27].

The sockets were made out of the redemption money. This is where the tabernacle proper was placed. It rested upon silver. It rested upon redemption. Every individual will have to personally accept the redemption that is in Christ Jesus. You have to pay the redemption price. What is it? Well, it is not silver or gold. The only condition is that you must be thirsty. Would you like to have a drink of the water of life? It is free. Salvation is free, but it is not cheap. It cost God everything. He gave His Son to die on the Cross and to pay the price of our redemption. We are redeemed by His blood.

In the wilderness, redemption was forced upon the nation of Israel. But when they got into the land, if they wanted to be numbered with the redeemed, they had to pay the price of redemption. Thank God it has already been paid for us. It does not cost any money. It does not have any price—but you must be thirsty for it. Do you want to be saved? Do you recognize that you have a need, that you are a sinner? Then come. The price has been paid. Christ has shed His precious blood for you. It enables you to come to God and to be accepted by Him through Christ.

CHAPTER 39

THEME: The holy garments of the high priest

Aaron was the high priest, and the garments he wore all spoke of the person of Christ. We have already been given the pattern for these garments.

> And of the blue, and purple, and scarlet, they made cloths of service, to do service in the holy place, and made the holy garments for Aaron; as the LORD commanded Moses.
>
> And he made the ephod of gold, blue, and purple, and scarlet, and fine twined linen [Exod. 39:1–2].

These garments are called "holy" because they are set apart for the service of God.

> And the curious girdle of his ephod, that was upon it, was of the same, according to the work thereof; of gold, blue, and purple, and scarlet, and fine twined linen; as the LORD commanded Moses [Exod. 39:5].

It was "curious" in the sense that it was woven in an unusual way. There were eight articles of clothing worn by the high priest. Four were the same or similar to those worn by all the priests. Four were peculiar to him and separated him from the other priests; they were "garments for glory and for beauty." This is a picture of our great High Priest, the Lord Jesus Christ, in all His extraordinary graces and glory. Each article of clothing was symbolic.

On the great Day of Atonement when Aaron took the blood into the Holy of Holies, he laid aside all of his garments of beauty and glory and wore only the simple linen garments that the other priests wore. He must be unadorned but pure.

The white linen that the priests wore speaks of righteousness. Isaiah 52:11 says, "Depart ye, depart ye, go ye out from thence, touch no unclean thing; go ye out of the midst of her; be ye clean, that bear the vessels of the LORD." God still says this. I do not believe that God uses a sinful preacher, teacher, or layman, no matter how prominent or talented he may be. They are doing nothing for God because He will not accept their work. They are building with wood, hay, and stubble. We must be clothed with the righteousness of Christ and then live a life to back it up. This is one lesson taught in these basic garments.

It is interesting to note that when Aaron went into the Holy of Holies to offer the sacrifice for the sin of the people, he laid aside his garments of glory and beauty. When the Lord Jesus came to earth, He did not lay aside His deity, but He did lay aside the garments of glory and beauty—that is, He laid aside His prerogatives as God. He laid aside the Shekinah glory and came to earth as a human being; He was born a baby. Man was looking for a king, not a baby. Then He offered Himself as a sacrifice for sin. He died in His humanity.

To say that God died on the Cross is not quite accurate. I wonder what they mean by "death." When Jesus Christ died on the Cross, He was separated from God, that is true. There was a rift in the Godhead, to be sure, when Christ was made sin for us who knew no sin (2 Cor. 5:21). But even at that moment, God was in Christ, reconciling the world unto Himself (2 Cor. 5:19). This is a mystery, friends, that I cannot penetrate. I have read the works of many theologians and have found that they have not penetrated it either.

These garments of beauty and glory were really lovely. The high priest was richly attired and colorful. He wore the ephod which had two stones, one on each shoulder, with six of the names of the tribes engraved on one stone and six on the other, which speaks of the strength and ability of our Lord, that Great Shepherd of the sheep. When one sheep gets lost, our Great Savior finds it, puts it on His shoulders and brings it back. Thank God that we have a Shepherd who can put us on His shoulders and bring us safely back to the fold. He is able to save to the uttermost all who come unto God through Him (Heb. 7:25).

The high priest also wore a breastplate which was somewhat like a vest. It had twelve stones on it, and it was a thing of great beauty. Possibly it had some sort of pocket where the Urim and Thummim were placed. The Urim and Thummim had something to do with prediction. We are not told how it worked. The beautiful stones on the breastplate speak of the fact that Christ carries us on His heart today. He loves us. "For God so loved the world, that He gave his only begotten Son, that whosoever believeth in him should not perish, but have everlasting life" (John 3:16). These stones depict His great love for us.

Now on the robe of the ephod were the golden bells and pomegranates so that when the high priest was serving, those bells could be heard ringing as he went into the Holy Place. The pomegranates speak of the fruitful life of the believer. The bells speak of the testimony of that life. When the priest was in the Holy Place, the Israelites could say, "Well, he is in there, in the place of worship, serving for us. We know he is there because we can hear the bells." That is what worship should mean to us, friend. Our high priest is representing us in God's presence. It ought to draw us to the person of Christ.

I used to have an elder in one of my churches when I was a young man who was a great encouragement to me. He was a wonderful man of God and he would come to me on Sunday morning and say, "Well, you rang the bell today." If you want to know the truth, I really did not. I preached some lousy sermons in those days but his point was, because he was a student of the Bible, that he was able to come into the presence of Christ through the preaching of the Word of God.

To hear the bells of the high priest was a wonderful experience. What a picture the garments of the priest give! The mitre on his head said, "HOLINESS UNTO THE LORD." This speaks of holiness and has to do with the inner life, but the important thing is that it means the high priest is wholly given to the work of the ministry. *Holy* means anything that is set aside for the use of God.

There is something I would like to say to preachers today. I have been a preacher for a long time now and I know there are a great many people who want a preacher to do everything under the sun. They want him to socialize, backslap, hold hands, be nursemaid, as well as preach. No wonder many preachers have nervous breakdowns. Many preachers are nothing more than wet nurses for a lot of little babies in

Christ. They go around burping them all the time. The preacher who stands in the pulpit today ought to be able to wear the mitre "HOLINESS UNTO THE LORD." That is, he should have time to prepare a message. He should have time to spend before God in prayer. I am amazed at the number of people who invite the preacher out on a Saturday night. That should be his day for meditation and preparation. I once had an elder say to me, "Vernon, I appreciate your coming to see me, but I will tell you what I would like you to do. I would like you to spend time preparing a message instead of visiting me. Business is difficult today, and I get weary and discouraged. When I come to church on Sunday, I want to hear something that comes from God. I need help and I hope you will spend Saturday preparing so that I will be able to hear from heaven on Sunday morning and evening."

I think he had a right to say that. My friend, we need to recognize the fact that preachers ought to wear the mitre. Without it, our ministry for the Lord will not be effective.

CHAPTER 40

THEME: The tabernacle erected and filled with the Shekinah glory

In this chapter the tabernacle is set up. I want to deal with only one thing because we have already dealt with every article of furniture and the garments of the priest. When Moses had the tabernacle set up in the camp of Israel, an amazing thing happened.

> Then a cloud covered the tent of the congregation, and the glory of the LORD filled the tabernacle.
>
> And Moses was not able to enter into the tent of the congregation, because the cloud abode thereon, and the glory of the LORD filled the tabernacle.
>
> And when the cloud was taken up from over the tabernacle, the children of Israel went onward in all their journeys:
>
> But if the cloud were not taken up, then they journeyed not till the day that it was taken up.
>
> For the cloud of the LORD was upon the tabernacle by day, and fire was on it by night, in the sight of all the house of Israel, throughout all their journeys [Exod. 40:34–38].

When the apostle Paul attempts to identify the Israelites in the Book of Romans, he enumerates several things that set them apart from other peoples. One was the *Shekinah* glory (Rom. 9:4). The Israelites were the only people to ever have the glory of God, the visible presence of God. That is what led them through the great and terrible wilderness. The cloud would lift in the morning if they were to journey that day. If it did not lift, the children of Israel stayed in the camp. They did not attempt to move that day. They never moved by their own wisdom or judgment. They did not vote on whether or not they should move, and Moses did not make the decision—the cloud did!

We sometimes say in our churches that Christ is the Head of the church. How about your church? Is He the Head of your church? Are we following the cloud today or do we put a man on the church board because he is a successful businessman? You hear people say today, "I want to talk to my preacher about this problem. I want him to tell me what to do." We who are pastors are not experts at telling people what they should do. We cannot solve everyone's marital problems. But there is a pillar of cloud today although most people do not see it. It is the Holy Spirit of God. He ought to be the One to lead us and guide us. Oh, how He is neglected! We are always appealing to someone human or something outside of God for help. But we need preachers, teachers, and laymen who are filled with the *Spirit* of God. Our churches need leaders who pay attention to the Word of God, and who want to do the will of God. There is no visible cloud over the church today, but the Holy Spirit of God wants to lead and guide us.

This concludes our studies in the Book of Exodus. It opened in the gloom of the brickyards of Egypt, and it closed in the glorious presence of the Lord in the tabernacle. It was His presence that led them through the wilderness. God wants to deliver you from the gloom of the slavery of sin and to bring you into the glory of His presence and into the very center of His will where He can lead and guide you. What a wonderful book is Exodus!

BIBLIOGRAPHY
(Recommended for Further Study)

Borland, James A. *Christ in the Old Testament*. Chicago, Illinois: Moody Press, 1978.

Davis, John J. *Moses and the Gods of Egypt*. Grand Rapids, Michigan: Baker Book House, 1971.

Epp, Theodore H. *Moses*. Lincoln, Nebraska: Back to the Bible Broadcast, 1975.

Gaebelein, Arno C. *Annotated Bible*. Vol. I. Neptune, New Jersey: Loizeaux Brothers, 1917.

Gispen, William Hendrik. *Exodus*. Grand Rapids, Michigan: Zondervan Publishing House, 1982.

Grant, F. W. *Numerical Bible*. Neptune, New Jersey: Loizeaux Brothers, 1891.

Gray, James M. *Synthetic Bible Studies*. Old Tappan, New Jersey: Fleming H. Revell Company, 1906.

Huey, F. B., Jr. *Exodus: Bible Study Commentary*. Grand Rapids, Michigan: Zondervan Publishing House, 1977.

Jensen, Irving L. *Exodus*. Chicago, Illinois: Moody Press, 1967.

Mackintosh, C. H. (C.H.M.). *Notes on the Pentateuch*. Neptune, New Jersey: Loizeaux Brothers, 1880.

McGee, J. Vernon. *The Tabernacle, God's Portrait of Christ*. Pasadena, California: Thru the Bible Books.

Meyer, F. B. *Exodus*. Grand Rapids, Michigan: Kregel Publications, 1952.

Meyer, F. B. *Moses: The Servant of God*. Fort Washington, Pennsylvania: Christian Literature Crusade, n.d.

Morgan, G. Campbell. *The Unfolding Message of the Bible*. Old Tappan, New Jersey: Fleming H. Revell Company.

Pink, Arthur W. *Gleanings in Exodus*. Chicago, Illinois: Moody Press, 1922.

Ridout, Samuel. *Lectures on the Tabernacle*. Neptune, New Jersey: Loizeaux Brothers, 1914.

Thomas W. H. Griffith. *Through the Pentateuch Chapter by Chapter*. Grand Rapids, Michigan: William B. Eerdmans Company, 1957.

Unger, Merrill F. *Unger's Bible Handbook*. Chicago, Illinois: Moody Press, 1966.

Unger, Merrill F. *Unger's Commentary on the Old Testament*, Vol. I. Chicago, Illinois: Moody Press, 1981.

Youngblood, Ronald F. *Exodus*. Chicago, Illinois: Moody Press, 1983.